Club
Operations and
Management

Club
Operations and
Management

Ted E. White
Florida International University

A CBI BOOK
Published by Van Nostrand Reinhold Company

A CBI BOOK
(CBI is an imprint of Van Nostrand Reinhold Company Inc.)

Copyright © 1979 by Van Nostrand Reinhold Company Inc.

Library of Congress Catalog Card Number 79-11864
ISBN 0-8436-0783-1

Printed in United States of America

Van Nostrand Reinhold Company Inc.
135 West 50th Street
New York, New York 10020

Van Nostrand Reinhold Company Limited
Molly Millars Lane
Wokingham, Berkshire RG11 2PY, England

Van Nostrand Reinhold
480 La Trobe Street
Melbourne, Victoria 3000, Australia

Macmillan of Canada
Division of Canada Publishing Corporation
164 Commander Boulevard
Agincourt, Ontario M1S 3C7, Canada

16 15 14 13 12 11 10 9 8 7 6 5 4 3 2

Library of Congress Cataloging in Publication Data

White, Ted, 1912-
    Club operations and management.

    Includes index.
    1. Clubs—Management. I. Title.
TX911.3.M27W45   658'.91'6479   79-11864
ISBN 0-8436-0783-1

Contents

Preface

The purpose of this text is to provide the reader with a ready reference to those details pertinent to club management. The book is not all-encompassing but rather the author's best estimate of the scope and complexities of the business and its problem areas.

The club business, with its cousins in all phases of the hospitality fields, is composed of a thousand-and-one small details; when overlooked these add up to large disasters. Therefore, this is a detail book, and as with all books it is a blend of the author's experience and education.

The intent of the author is to provide, under one cover, a comprehensive work that can be used as a text for students and/or handbook for inexperienced managers. It is hoped that it would also provide the very talented and experienced manager with a checklist and perhaps a new or different method for solving any of the myriad problems that are peculiar to this profession.

Ted E. White
Miami, Florida

1

History

OVERVIEW

This chapter will introduce the reader to "clubs"—an integral part of the hospitality business. The meaning and purpose of clubs are defined, and some of the history of the profession is reviewed.

The role of the Club Manager's Association of America (CMAA), in relation to managerial professionalism, is traced from its beginning to the present time.

The role of the club manager is discussed in general, and in connection with the temptations and pitfalls of the business.

PROBLEMS

The "club," an integral part of the hospitality industry, has been ignored for too long. The management of clubs has been considered a servile position by hotel people. Very few clubs have had the organizational structure to spotlight the club business by doing things that hotel chains could do. This includes financing the Statler Inn at Cornell University, the Hilton at the University of Houston, and many others. Until the late 1960s, when a chain of clubs was started in Texas and one in California, clubs were single financial entities and stayed out of the limelight.

Clubs, however, collectively constitute an important segment of the hospitality industry and employ a host of management personnel with salaries and job satisfactions that hotels and restaurants cannot hope to match. The club manager has a variety of management responsibilities that cover the full spectrum of the business. Many clubs include bars, cocktail lounges, party rooms, and many other activities as well as multiple types of feeding operations. These can include complete athletic facilities, theatres, hotel rooms, gymnasiums, and shops. In addition, the private club has some very unique legal, financial, and tax problems that management must handle.

DEFINITION

A "club" is any gathering of selective, specific humans in a defined, delineated place for any social or recreational activity. Size, per se, does not affect this definition. Four ladies gathered at one home to play bridge is a "bridge club" if they so desire to designate it as one. A five-thousand membership country club meeting on a ten-million-dollar property can also be a club. As long as the social and recreational significance is maintained, reasons for membership do not matter. If one joins a club for a recreational or social reason, or to sell real estate, stocks and bonds, insurance, or seeks promotion in or for his company on the golf course, this is accepted.

The key words in determining when a gathering is a club is that a selective process of some kind for determining membership was used. This could mean a membership-committee selection, such as a country club might use or a regulatory provision that business, faculty, or military clubs rely on.

However, as the purpose of this book is to provide management guidance, the types of clubs to be considered are those that own or rent property where the volume of activity warrants a manager.

ORIGINS

The first clubs in ancient Greece and the Roman Empire were political in nature, very exclusive in membership and usually revolved around the communal baths. They provided relaxation, privacy, and membership separation of the sexes. A favored slave was usually the manager and the employees, both male and female, were selected from the household slave staff. In addition to their other duties, slaves were required to be prostitutes for the members. The emphasis was on total relaxation and privacy for members. Much of the government's behind-the-scenes business was conducted at the baths: plots were conjured, assassinations planned, and influences swapped. The conduct at times was quite scandalous and altogether different from the life style of the barbarous counties. But it was so attractive that the phrase "when in Rome, do as the Romans do" was probably coined and used as a conscience balm during these times.

Another type of club business was originated by the Greek armies in the field. Military leadership, usually reserved for royalty, eventually came to be decided as much on ability in action as on inheritance. A Greek general is thought to be responsible for using the word "mesa" to indicate men of equal rank dining together from a common pot. The meals usually continued into social functions. Mess, a corruption of this word "mesa," was widely used in medieval times to describe the sharing of a meal by military groups. (The American Armed Forces inherited the word from the British, and clubs in the Army, Navy, Marine Corps, Air Force, and Coast Guard used the term until 1976 or 77 when the forces, with the exception of the Navy and Air Force, shifted to the word club.)

BIBLICAL INFLUENCE

The Bible is responsible for a step in club history. It created a meaningful title for the manager of an activity, which has been translated as steward. The title was first used in the Gospel of John to describe a man who is in charge of a household and its myriad duties and responsibilities. Then again in Luke, the steward is mentioned and his duties are described. It is important to understand that while this man was always a slave and a servant, he was also the manager of his domain.

The understanding of the word steward is very important. The term is still used by many transportation services (airlines and ships) to indicate that person who is in charge or serves food. This is not a proper title for the club manager and is no longer used by professionals.

EARLY TWENTIETH CENTURY

Clubs in the late nineteenth century and the early twentieth century were the exclusive preserves of the rich. Membership was the social "in thing." Clubs were used primarily in America to preserve the exclusiveness of communal recreation spaces. As most homes were, in reality, mansions requiring a full-service staff, the club members equated the club employees with their own butlers, cooks, and maids. Some managers were treated as professionals and had the esteem and respect of the members; but many were treated as servants.

MODERN TIMES

A powerful force, however, started working to remove the servant image of managers, changing it to a professional one. In 1927 the Club Managers Association of America (CMAA) was formed. At this time in America, clubs numbered about ten-thousand entities, forty-five hundred city and fifty-five hundred country. A group of progressive managers met in Chicago to start their organization. As women have always been an integral part of the club management, it is interesting to note that nine women attended this organizational meeting.

Country club membership in the period between the two world wars was reserved for the more affluent of our society. The "jet set" was the in group in the 60s; in the 20s and 30s it was the "country club set." Clubs stayed very low-key with rigidly controlled public relations and powerful, arrogant membership committees. These committees carefully screened every application (the submitting of which, in many cases, required tremendous influence) and thus kept the clubs exclusive. This, however, gradually eroded. The millionaires were separated from the six-figure people, and they in turn from the five-figure people. The first real breakthrough in the caste systems of clubs started in the late 30s when business, stimulated by the wars in Europe and Asia, overflowed from the boardrooms to the clubs. It then became necessary to open membership to new and working money so as to provide a continuity of business meetings.

It is an interesting part of club history that the mass-produced automobile made clubs more exclusive—they allowed the old line city clubs to expand into the country with little inconvenience to the members.

The Club Managers Association of America, now with over 3000 members, is celebrating its fiftieth anniversary. It constantly strives to improve the professional image of the manager. Membership is open to all professional managers regardless of race, color, or creed. The Association has a rigid code of ethics that its members must adhere to and that has gained its membership the respect of the hospitality industry.

CERTIFIED CLUB MANAGER

The CMAA also offers its members a certification program. The professional, experienced, educated, and successful manager may earn certification through the Association by active participation in its programs. It is accepted by the industry as the benchmark of professional knowledge and competence. The CCM (Certified Club Manager) after a club manager's name indicates full acceptance of his or her proficiency. In the years to come this will probably become the one single factor that prospective employers will insist upon for candidates for management positions.

Club management as a career provides more opportunity for individual management initiative than any other facet of the hospitality profession. Innovative thinking must become routine as the challenge of change is constant.

The members, through dues, pay for the privilege of using the club. Thus they have a right to expect they will be offered different and better fare than the best restaurant in town, as well as expecting good drinks served properly, in the right atmosphere. In short, they should receive the manager's full attention, their desires and needs met with a full provision of the basic hospitality niceties. They, however, do not have the right to expect the manager to be a servant.

ETHICS AND RATIONALE

The CMAA prescribes that a club manager adhere to certain standards of conduct. Some of these are listed here.

It shall be incumbent upon club managers to be knowledgeable in the application of sound business principles in the management of clubs. Ample opportunities are available through CMAA to keep abreast of current practices and procedures.

Club managers shall be judicious in their relationship with club members, aware of the need to maintain a line of professional demarcation between manager and the club membership. This is a fine line and it must be seriously considered to avoid involvements that can only lead to misunderstanding and censure.

Club managers shall set an example by their demeanor and behavior that employees can use as a guide in their contact with club members and guests. This is an area that requires controlled familiarity between employees and the club manager.

Club managers shall serve the community in every way possible by being cooperative and helpful; they should maintain good relations with all segments of the public sector and actively participate in community affairs to the extent possible within the limits of their clubs' demands.

Club managers shall pursue their quest for knowledge through educational seminars and meetings that will improve their ability to manage their clubs.

Club managers shall actively participate in local and national association meetings and activities. They should maintain the prestige of their professional status and at the same time make a contribution to the organization.

Club managers shall be above reproach. There can be no half measure of integrity, in their obligations to their clubs, their employees, their club members, or in their dealings with purveyors. Honesty in all transactions—in time, money, and expenditures—is a basic requisite; misappropriation or the acceptance of subsidies can only result in maligning the professional standing of the members of the association.

Club managers shall be ready at all times to offer assistance to their associates, their club officials and all others engaged in the maintenance and conduct of their club operations.

Club managers shall conduct themselves in a manner that will bring credit to the profession. In their personal association with club officials and members of the board of trustees they will be considerate of the club's well-being.

Club managers shall not be deterred from compliance with the law as it applies to their club. They have an obligation to provide their club officers and trustees with the specifics of federal, state, and local laws, statutes, and regulations, to avoid punitive action and costly litigation.

It is unfortunate that not all club managers adhere to these professional standards that are so desperately needed in the industry, but then all doctors are not healers and not all lawyers espouse justice. There was and is a "white-collar mafia" as well as a "khaki" one.

Equally bad are those managers without the knowledge or will to state their moral positions when they are directed by the club board of directors to do things that are wrong. The pitfalls are many; special prices and favors for a selected few, outright bribery by managers to keep their jobs, and favors by selected vendors.

The manager must view his position as one based on trust. He must protect the assets of the club from internal, as well as external, subversion. The interest of young, talented, and aware people in the club business will eventually make this a career to be envied. Perhaps the title of manager has become as passé as the five-cent phone call. More than likely the title will be changed in the near future to a more meaningful one. Certainly the club manager has greater authority and responsibility

The practice greens make a beautiful entrance to the Club.

than his peers in comparable industries and the title should reflect the position. Many clubs have already added "general" to the title of manager, indicating that this person has overall responsibility and authority for the operation. Many more title changes are in the offing and will probably be along the lines of "director" or "executive director of club operations."

Today, clubs are a multi-million-dollar growth business that is as much a part of the American dream as the forty-hour week. People are finding out they have a need to get away from the exclusive family environment (not to mention television sets!) and mix with a homogenous group in a recreational setting. The American worker has more leisure time and more leisure dollars than ever before. It is up to the entire club industry to give this worker the opportunity to put a club in his recreation future.

REVIEW QUESTIONS

1. Of what importance is the study of ancient and modern history of clubs to today's manager?

2. Does the definition of a club clearly separate it from other social gatherings?
3. What is the history of the word "steward" as a job title, and where may it be properly applied today?
4. Define the rationale for "standards of conduct;" are they unique in the club management profession?
5. Are the "standards of conduct" published by the CMAA realistic in today's moral climite?
6. What role has the CMAA played in the club field?
7. What is the potential growth of the club business in the immediate future?

2

The Club

OVERVIEW

The aim of this chapter is to introduce various types of clubs from the standpoint of both functional and financial management.

The internal management structure of various clubs is examined to illustrate the differences in control between private and membership-owned entities. The various positions of control and management relationships that pivot on this control are explained.

The duties of each person and committee in control are clarified so that there is an observable management chain. A suggested organization chart is presented.

The duties and responsibilities of the club manager are spelled out so that each one may be diagnosed.

TYPES OF CLUBS

Following our definition in chapter 1, the term "club" as used in this text means any organization large enough to require a manger. Clubs are usually named for their physical natures.

Bowling teams sponsored by the Club are very popular, either at the Club or at a commercial lane.

There are many different kinds of clubs and many subtypes within the kinds. Some are listed here.

Country Clubs

These clubs consist of buildings and grounds spacious enough to have at least a golf course, swimming pool, and tennis courts. An eighteen-hole regulation golf course needs at least 118 acres of land, thus the name "country club" because acreage in such amounts is usually found on the outskirts of cities. The older country clubs, which cities have eventually surrounded usually traded their land (at great financial gain) and moved into suburbia. In addition to the three main recreational activities country clubs may also offer:

- horse-back riding, sometimes including stabling services for members animals
- diving, wading, and child's pools

Many Clubs use peripheral roads to encourage cycling activities.

- driving and putting ranges
- archery, rifle, skeet, and pistol ranges
- bicycling lanes
- skating rinks
- jogging paths
- bocci and lawn bowling courts
- cross country skiing
- deck and paddle tennis courts
- squash and handball courts
- volleyball courts
- track and field facilities
- television lounges
- billiard rooms
- card rooms
- exercise rooms
- sauna and steam rooms

The Club teaching and driving range attracts members of all ages.

City Clubs

These clubs are usually in a city and have all their activities in one building or part of one building. Both the Press Club in Washington and the Commerce Club in Atlanta occupy one or more floors of an office building. They will usually have a restaurant, bar and cocktail lounge, television lounges, billiard rooms, and some athletic facilities. Many have indoor swimming pools, squash and handball courts, card rooms, and bowling lanes.

Yacht Clubs

These clubs, located on a body of water, have docks, mooring buoys, etc., and may or may not have a full-service club house. They have gas pumps, oil, water, and electricity and many have sewerage connection facilities that can handle direct flow on holding tanks. Their primary concern is boating—power, (man or motor), sailing, or all three.

Fraternal Clubs

These are the membership clubs such as the Elks, Masons, American Legion, Veterans of Foreign Wars, etc. who own or rent but operate their own facility. They usually offer a restaurant, bar and cocktail lounge, television lounge, billiard rooms, and card rooms. Some of the larger ones may even offer services similar to those of a city club. Because of their political clout many have slot machines and other gaming devices in states where such devices are not legal. This is a major source of revenue and allows the clubs to offer amenities that other clubs cannot match.

Government Clubs

These clubs are run by the various departments of the Government. Through the Army, Navy, Marines, and Air Force, the Department of Defense runs many clubs. Other government departments such as the Departments of State and Agriculture also operate clubs. The facilities offered members are comparable to those offered by the country and city types of clubs.

The subtypes of clubs constitute businesses that have some type of recreational facility as an integral part and may be represented by the "club" definition concept.

Condominium and Apartment Complex Clubs

All types of recreational activities are now included in the larger complexes. The manager must have a working knowledge of the club business. Many have swimming pools, tennis courts, restaurants, bar and cocktail lounges, and other amenities that require control and management. This concept is new but growing as more demand is established for "one-stop living."

Retirement Apartments and Hotels

These offer meals as part of the monthly rent and require professional management. The meal can be breakfast, luncheon, or dinner in any combination, or all three. In addition, they may have card rooms, television lounges, and pool tables. The dining room is usually multiple in function where entertainment (such as theatre acts, plays, and motion pictures) may be shown for the occupants.

Speciality Clubs

Clubs large enough to require a manager but usually do not have a clubhouse are specialty clubs, such as a swim, tennis, golf, or polo club.

TYPES OF OWNERSHIP

Two types of ownership are membership and commercial club organization. The club may be located on its own or rental property and its financial and management organization can be anyone of several. The financial structure has a vast effect on its operation; each must be understood.

Membership Owned

The arrangement here, as the name implies, has the financial ownership split among the members, as a corporation or as a very loosely organized partnership. If it is a corporation, the value of the stock issued can equal the original value of the investment or its current value, expressed either as an initiation or an admission fee. A constitution or set of bylaws are used as policy guidance. The membership elects a president and a board of directors. They in turn hire a manager and appoint standing and special committees. Monthly or annual dues are charged. The constitution or bylaws focus on three areas: officers, membership, and finances. The officers have complete control over who may join and what the costs will be. Although usually set up as nonprofit organizations allowing for specific tax breaks, through professional management most of these clubs work very successfully.

Commercially Owned

Commercially owned clubs make up the other type of civilian clubs. Although those who join pay an initiation fee and monthly dues, these are clubs not owned by the membership. The owners usually allow the members to elect a president and officers, but in most instances will serve as a board of directors and hire the manager. A very large segment of the commercially owned clubs are an attraction for real-estate sales. Presented as either a profit or nonprofit organization, a country club will be built by a developer as part of the overall real-estate come-on. Home buyers then pay little or no initiation fees and nominal monthly dues to use these clubs. The problem develops when all the houses in the subdivision are sold and the builder no longer needs the club to promote sales. The original cost of the club and expenses for the estimated time it will take to sell the houses is part of the sales price. Now the club, because of the low dues structure has some options on what can be done to eliminate this operational expense. These are:

1. Close it. This is the hardest way as such action will probably be challenged with law suits, the reason being that the club was used as part of the sales agreement.

2. Get a management company to operate it. This is relatively easy if there is a broad patron base and a profit possibility. One California company now has nineteen operational contracts and is growing at a rate of one or two units a month. There are also two very successful Texas companies.

3. Sell it. Finding a single or corporate buyer who would invest in this high risk business is very difficult, but possible. Selling to the membership is easier, however. The members will usually buy the club if it is successful and the sale can be accomplished with no money down. The owner will be a long time regaining his investment but this is the most common way that privately owned clubs attached to development projects are moved. If the property is mortgaged the developer must arrange for the members to assume this obligation, usually meaning he will have to guarantee the transaction. If the property is unencumbered the developer can make his own deal. He can take a percentage of sales, initiation fees, etc. to get his money out, but it is a long drawn out process nevertheless.

INTERNAL MANAGEMENT STRUCTURE

Clubs are internally management structured by establishing a constitution and bylaws. These establish election procedures, officer positions, a board of directors, and standing committees. Guidance and direction are also provided as to what and how each office and committee will function. The constitution states the broader policy with the bylaws containing the details.

The membership is given the authority by the constitution to elect the officers and/or directors of the club whose sole function is to represent the membership by establishing the policy under which the club will operate. It is a good idea to have last year's president continue as a director, providing continuity of management.

The number of elected officers is determined by the size and number of functioning activities. The number of directors depends on the representative needs of the membership. The entire group, the officers and directors, is called the board of directors.

Officers

The outline of officers and officer positions is as follows:

President. The president is someone the membership believes is the most qualified person to lead the club through the coming year. Many times the members mistake popularity with ability and the manager will be in for a very bad time. The president, however, will have a lot of authority and the manager will have to work along with him or her, or leave. One way to make the manager's job easier is to train the president. CMAA has done a tremendous job in stressing the manager's importance to the president by means of a booklet called "Mr. President."

The president will preside at all official meetings and will be the leader in policy making and guidance. The president should be the final authority in all policy and management matters. He or she thus becomes a force for both good and bad procedures.

His or her respect or lack of it for the manager will determine whether or not a successful team will be formed.

Vice-president. The vice-president performs all of the president's duties in his or her absence. The vice-president can also be appointed chairperson of a committee. There may also be more than one vice-president. In this case, precedence would be controlled by numbering them first, second, etc.

Treasurer. The treasurer will normally be versed in financial matters and can provide advice and guidance for the monetary systems of the club. This person should engage an audit firm for the annual or biannual audits, work with the manager on control of cash flow, and be aware of the control systems for cash that the manager has installed. The treasurer may also be appointed the chairperson of a committee.

Secretary. The secretary will record the minutes of meetings, take care of the club-related correspondence for the officers and board of directors, and have other clerical, supervisory duties. This position is often combined with that of the treasurer in which case the officer is then called the secretary-treasurer. The secretary may also be a chairperson of a committee.

Sergeant-at-Arms. This person will normally be an expert on *Robert's Rules of Order* and will advise the president at meetings on procedural matters. Also one of the duties of office may be keeping order at all meetings.

Committees

A committee is a group of members who voluntarily serve to provide policy and guidance on one particular aspect of the club's business.

The president of the club and/or the board of directors will appoint the chairpersons for each committee. The chairperson alone or with the appointing authority will appoint the committee members. In most clubs these positions carry a great deal of prestige and it is comparatively easy to find volunteers. Care should be taken, however, to suit the individual to the job. A golfer will usually head up the golf committee as a nongolfer might, in this position, do great harm to the club image.

The committees system works when the members stick to policy making, and taking advice and guidance from the professional manager, while allowing the manager full control of the day-to-day operations.

Some of the most popular committees are:

Finance and/or budget committees
House committee
Membership committee
Entertainment committee
Selected sports committees
Athletic committee
Special committees

The special committees are formed for a one-time reason or function and then disbanded with a letter of thanks. For example, the entertainment committee may decide that the club will have a dinner theatre on a particular night. They may work with the manager to put on the affair or may appoint a special committee to handle it.

The following broad rules on committees may be of assistance:

1. The membership is limited. Three is an ideal number with one member as chairperson. There is an old axiom "if you want to delay a project indefinitely refer it to a large committee." Unfortunately, the club committee carries a great amount of prestige and the chairperson usually equates the importance of the committee in direct ratio to the number of members.

2. They set policy only and are governed by detailed instructions in the constitution and bylaws. A committee member should only address the manager on instructions, direction, or problems. A professional manager does not allow the committee to supervise his staff.

3. They seek advice and guidance from the manager.

4. They understand and establish "standing and special committees," sometimes known as one-function or ad hoc. The standing or permanent committees are usually determined by the size and principle activities of the club.

5. Committees perform when there is a policy to determine who makes

the final decisions in a disagreement. Matters may be referred back to an officer (the president, etc.), to the full board of directors, or to the total membership.

6. The manager works with the committees but reports to one officer. By working for just one person a line of authority can be established. This gives the manager the options and freedom of action that is needed.
7. The club could purchase a supply of "So You're on a Committee" and distribute to all new members. This pamphlet is published by CMMA, 7615 Winterberry Place, P.O. Box 34482, Washington, D.C., 20034.

Committee Functions

Financial and/or Budget Committee. This committee has only one duty, to ensure the club remains solvent. They work closely with the manager and do this in many ways. The most acceptable are:

1. Determine the cost of the operation of each department. This is done by management submitting an operating budget.
2. Determine the percentage of "self-sufficiency" for each department. For example, will the dining room be required to make money, break even, or be subsidized? Will the golf course be 25, 50, or 100 percent self-sufficient?
3. Determine how subsidies will be met. The options are (after the fee charges) dues, assessments, percentages of concession profits, and capital. Management must keep the committee informed as to the latest financial thinking in the industry. For example, paid professionals who also get exclusive sales rights in pro retail shops are more and more a luxury that many clubs can no longer afford.
4. Establish the financing and approval policy with the manager for a capital improvements and refurbishment budget, prepared by the house committee.

House Committee. This committee is responsible for the condition of the physical plant. The plant must be able to provide the facilities for the operation. The committee is consulted on expansion, renovation, new furnishings, equipment, and all related subjects.

They, with the manager, will prepare one, five, and ten year "capital improvements budgets" for submission to the finance committee.

This committee can be given many other duties, some can even be operational, but usually they are limited to judgments on policy in relation to things not people.

Membership Committee. This committee's duties are connected with the members in that they control admission and the member's moral and physical conduct. They usually prepare the application form and format, and rule on the admissibility of each candidate. They normally have the authority to withdraw as well as grant the membership privileges. This is where racism, religious bigotry, and financial status symbols play a large role, if the membership allows it.

They can be of tremendous help to the manager in dealing with member problems. A good membership committee will set the tone for the club officers and other committees. The three trouble areas for the manager are abuse of employees, theft, and financial irresponsibility.

Entertainment Committee. This committee is responsible for the entertainment policy of the club.They must know the entertainment wishes of the membership and plan to respond to them. They should act as a "critics" panel for the manager and assist him in every way.

In some clubs, entertainment also includes the tournaments and other functions of the various sports committees. This is to be avoided if possible as it is more efficient for the sports committees to work directly with management.

Selected Sports Committees. These committees will control the operational policies of their particular responsibilities. The golf committee, for example, controls the operational policies for the course, the locker room, and related activities. They would usually be consulted in the hiring of key personnel and in preparing the golf course budget. They assist in the preparation and operation of all tournaments and oversee the conduct of all golfers while they are engaged in the sport.

This committee would develop the services to be offered members such as golf carts, lockers, shoe, club and ball cleaning, club repairs, pro shop operation, etc.

They would control starting-time procedures, handicap

computation, and decide when the course will be closed due to inclement weather, repairs, etc. They would also schedule and be responsible for the operation of all tournaments.

A large club might have committees for golf, tennis, swimming, cycling, horse-back riding, racquet ball, track and field, yacht racing, yacht sailing, etc, each with its own rules and regulations under the club constitution and bylaws.

Athletic Committee. This committee should have broad policy-making authority over a variety of sports. It is often used in city-club management to control all individual sports in a gymnasium. In a very small club it can substitute for individual sports committees and can work very well. In larger clubs, however, each sport and activity has its own committee.

Special Committees. These are used by every type of club. Controlling them is difficult because the line is so fine between policy and operation that they tend to take up management functions on many occasions. It takes a very strong professional manager to tell the chairperson of the "Mother's Day Committee" that while it might have been a good idea if planned, he can't order the waiters to dance with mothers who look lonesome.

The Manager

A professional manager must be the boss of the club. A chain of command may be established, but the person in complete charge of the day-to-day operation must be the manager.

The usual management relationship with the president, other club officers, committees, and groups is close cooperation and coordination. Their contact with the operating staff must be kept at an absolute minimum to achieve a smooth functioning organization. (See Exhibit 2-1.)

The club should be organized so that the manager discusses management with the officers, committees, and groups but only takes orders from the president. This is a prestige symbol for the manager that will definitely have beneficial effects in dealing with both the members and club employees.

The manager organizes the club into operational departments and if the size of the operation warrants it, has one or

Exhibit 2-1. Management Organization Chart

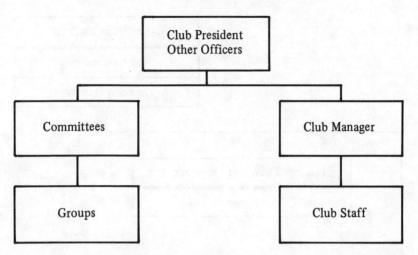

more assistants. A properly organized business will have from one to five persons reporting directly to the manager—the fewer, the better. The operation will not function efficiently if more than five persons report directly.

The manager's responsibilities as seen in Exhibit 2–2 are numerous and varied. To perform them competently, the manager must have training and ability. The finest training for management positions is a mix of academic and job experience. The duties that the manager may be called upon to do are:

- supervise the day-to-day operation of the club
- control the hiring, promotion, and dismissal of all employees
- assign the duties to all employees through position descriptions—this applies to the assistant manager, department heads, supervisors, and through all employees
- be responsible for the safety of all employees and their safe working conditions
- be responsible for developing a fringe benefit program for all employees—this can include, but not be limited to:

Leave of absence
Medical insurance
Group life insurance

Exhibit 2-2a. Operational Organization Chart

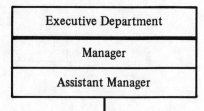

Executive Department
Manager
Assistant Manager

Food and Beverage Department
Manager

Recreation Department

Retail Sales Department
Retail Sales Manager

Support Department
Comptroller

Maintenance Department
Maintenance Superintendent

Exhibit 2-2b. Operational Organization Chart

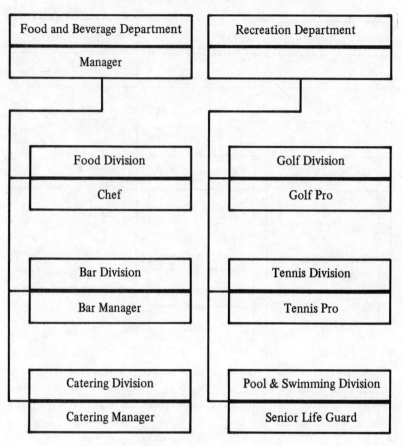

Retirement insurance
Disability insurance
Accident insurance

- be responsible for developing an in-house training and a career development program
- be responsible for all records and physical property of the club and for their safekeeping
- be responsible for all the cash and inventory of the club and for their safekeeping

Exhibit 2-2c. Operational Organization Chart

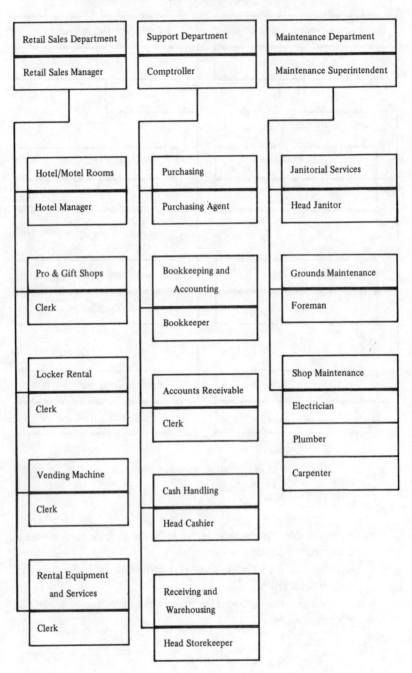

- sign checks and all financial documents
- prepare the necessary budgets and sales forecasts
- work closely with all committees, both standing and special, to supervise the club's insurance program, establish the hours of operation for all departments, and conrol all construction, maintenance, and refurbishment projects

Club Departments

A club is organized into divisions or departments for efficient operation. If these have individual persons in charge, it is advisable to limit their number. The reason for the limitation is that each must report to the manager; and more persons whom the manager must work with, the more difficult and time-consuming the position becomes. He or she must manage through the department and/or division heads.

A sound organizational structure is detailed in Exhibit 2–2.

REVIEW QUESTIONS

1. Name the various types of clubs that are listed in the text and define the objectives of each.
2. Discuss the two principle types of club ownership and the reason why a club may change from private to member owned.
3. Discuss the problems a privately owned club may have in selling it.
4. Discuss the types and objectives of the club committees.
5. Discuss the duties of the manager and his relationship with the club officers and committees.
6. Analyze the suggested departmental structure for the club. Explain the lines of authority for each department.

3

The Physical

Organization

of the Club

OVERVIEW

This chapter aims to detail a systematic approach to internal management organization, which in turn assists in determining the physical layout of the club.

The efficiency of proper organization, layout, and equipment used for each department to attain the maximum functionality is described.

The importance of having the necessary equipment and training personnel in its use is emphasized. The essential accouterments in all departments are discussed, and management options are explained.

The reader is encouraged to compare various techniques with those now being used, while being shown ways to make effective changes.

DEPARTMENTS

The internal organization of the club usually necessitates departmentalization. Such structuring assists good management in several ways. It details income and expenses, facilitating better control of profit or loss; pinpoints responsibilities for both management and operational personnel; refines budgeting and other planning.

The club may have separate departments for everything they do, or there can be many combinations. Good management practices, however, dictate that departments be established where there is income and expenses or one group working in multiple areas such as support systems and maintenance (bookkeeping, clerical, purchasing, clean-up and repairs).

The physical organization of a typical large club, with their divisions and sections, might be as follows:

Food and Beverage

Food Division: preparation section—control of all food; service section

Bar and Cocktail Lounge Division: preparation section—control of all beverages; service section

Catering Division: planning section; service section

Recreation

Golf Division: play and tournaments; lessons; technical maintenance

Tennis Division: play and tournaments; lessons; technical maintenance

Pool & Swimming Division: swimming, diving, and lessons; swimming meets; technical maintenance

Sauna and Steam Rooms

Miscellaneous

Retail Sales

Hotel/Motel Rooms: front desk; housekeeping

Pro and Gift Shops Divison: golf, tennis, swimming, and gift shops; locker rentals; rental equipment and service carts;

clubs, rental, cleaning, and repairs; vending machines; coin-operated devices

Support Systems

Purchasing
Bookkeeping and Accounting
Record Maintenance
Payroll
Cost Controls
Budgets
Accounts Receivable
Cash Handling
Receiving and Warehousing

Maintenance

Janitorial Services: cleaning; interior maintenance; party and other furniture setups
Grounds Maintenance: all exterior grounds including non-technical area; courts and pool
Shop Maintenance: electrician; plumber; carpenter

Food and Beverage Departments

In many clubs the food and bar operation will be in the same department, in others they will be separate. Sales volume should be the determining factor that defines the supervision necessary. The number of departments reporting directly to the manager must be kept to the absolute economic minimum if the manager is to do an efficient job. It usually does not make any difference in the physical layout if the departments are individual or combined, as the production is the same.

The manager may never get the opportunity to participate in the layout and design of the operational departments but a working knowledge of some of the principles involved will be important in using the facilities.

Food Division—Preparation Section

In starting any kitchen planning a number of things must be known. Some of these are: (1) what's on the menu; (2) how many people will be served; (3) where will it be served to the customer; (4) what space is available; and (5) how much money is budgeted? In the club business a full menu is usually served from the kitchen, with some satellite fast-food operations at the swimming pool or golf course. Also many clubs serve food in four styles: full table service, buffet, cafeteria, and to individuals as room service.

This information is used to determine the type, size, and placement of the equipment that will be needed. We will assume that the ideal plan is for raw-food materials to enter the building, be received, be placed in holding equipment, removed, prepared, and served to the customer. The necessary equipment and its placement is very important in achieving an overall product flow.

Starting with a receiving area as close to the kitchen entrance as possible, plan the raw-food holding areas—refrigerators, deep freezers, and dry holding areas (these are never called storage areas—resalable items are not stored but held until used). If desirable, the groceries room can be divided further into edible and nonedible sections, which then provide defined spaces for linen, china, silver, etc. Door opening should always be designed for the convenience of the kitchen staff not the storekeeper or delivery persons (i.e., door handles are placed on the side toward the kitchen preparation area). Not only does this save time but it is a positive security measure as items coming out of holding areas can more readily be seen from the kitchen.

The next step in the food production line could be to any one of four places:

1. to a sink with working drainboard; here vegetables might be prepared for both cooking and raw use
2. to a working table; here meats might be cut, frozen products unboxed and ingredients from holding spaces assembled
3. to the food preparation equipment; precut steaks might go directly to the broiler working table, cold meats to the meat slicer, and bacon and eggs to the range working table
4. to the service pantry; this might include ice cream, some breads, fresh fruit, and other items that require no equipment preparation

In planning along these lines it is possible to produce a food-production movement aisle. Management must think progressive, if the club industry is ever going to raise restaurant production above the one hour paid for 30 to 40 minutes work, and inspect typical "blind spots" such as these:

- having huge, high-ceiling kitchens
- crowding all the equipment that needs venting together under one hood; this results in all work tables being opposite the equipment
- planning wide aisles
- placing the dish room, including the machine, close to the dining area, and having the cooks wash pots and pans
- thawing all food before cooking
- planning to hand-carry items between points on the food production line
- not designing for "human scale"
- maintaining equipment that is no longer being used, such as meat saws, potato peeler, sixty- and eighty-gallon kettles, or huge ovens
- maintaining compressors and other types of equipment that must have remote power units placed in the kitchen
- overlooking necessary labor-saving equipment
- using ovens without fans

The size of the kitchen will depend on the products it must produce. The construction cost for unnecessary square feet is minimal compared to the daily cost of production, labor, and maintenace. The size of the dining area, in a club with service to tables, determines the square feet needed in the kitchen. Otherwise Parkinson's Law ("If space is available it will be used") will prevail. A good rule of thumb is as follows: Compute the square footage of:

- 60 percent of permanent dining spaces
- 20 percent of party and special dining rooms
- 10 percent of preparation spaces in satellite food operations

For example:

2000 sq. ft (267.73 sq. m) for dining room

1500 sq. ft. (200.36 sq. m) for party and special dining rooms, and
400 sq. ft. (53.49 sq. m) of snack bar will mean . . .

60% of 2000 = 1200 sq. ft. (160.24 sq. m) for kitchen
20% of 1500 = 300 sq. ft. (40.12 sq. m) for kitchen
10% of 400   = 40 sq. ft. (5.30 sq. m) for kitchen
1540 sq. ft. (260.15 sq. m) for total kitchen area

The basic preparation area of twelve hundred square feet is ample and will satisfy the needs of delivery and receiving, raw-food holding, preparation, cooking and baking, prepared-food holding and serving, plus dish, pot, and pan washing. The three hundred additional square feet for banquets, etc. is required to place and store the additional equipment needs, and also as a plating area. The forty square feet for the snack bar provides for "commissary" type food preparation, such as slicing and pre-packaging meats or other products.

The height of the kitchen ceiling should never exceed ten feet. Suspended ceilings, can hide pipes and structural beams. This has many advantages. It looks nicer, is cooler, cuts down on the noise, and it is easier to clean. There are new materials for suspended ceilings over work areas that can be taken down for cleaning.

It is no longer necessary to crowd all of the equipment under a hood. In some instances this seriously diminishes the efficiency of the kitchen. Many pieces of flat equipment such as ranges, fryers, and broilers can be self-ventilating, therefore they can be grouped to form the food-production line. Some companies manufacture venting hoods that act as passover shelves. This allows working tables to be placed next to all flat types of equipment. The increase in efficiency by having a work table beside a grill, rather than across an aisle, could be as high as 25 percent. With in-front-opening equipment, such as ovens and steamers, table areas must still be across the aisle. Aisles, however, can be narrow.

If employees are working on only one side of an aisle, 30 inches is sufficient; with employees on both sides add 6 inches. If carts need to be used in the aisles 48 inches in needed. The ideal arrangement is to have a 48-inch aisle running in a straight line from the raw-food holding area to the dining room. Every area in the kitchen then becomes a branch off this main corridor.

The dish room containing the solid-dish table, the garbage-disposal grinder, the dish machine, and one or more dish operators is noisy, wet, and steamy. Whenever possible this room should be against an outside wall with the sound baffled away from the dining room and kitchen work area. The optimum circular flow line is one from dish room to food-plating area, to the customer, back to dish room. With the availability of the *Lowrator* and other custom-made dish carts that can be used for holding clean dishes, glasses, and silver as well as transporting, two-thirds of the circle will not involve the dish room locale. The problem is really transporting the soiled dishes from the customer to the dish room. Many designers solve this problem by placing the dish room to the right of the egress from the dining room to the kitchen. Kitchens often have the dish machine on a wall separating the dining room from the kitchen. This arrangement solves one problem but creates many others. Ideally the dish room should be on the right, away from the dining room wall, with a sound-baffle wall constructed around the dish room, one door for employees and carts, and a pass-through for soiled eating gear and pots and pans.

One common error in many design plans is to have the pot and pan washing area close to the equipment where they are needed. This generally means that the persons using them will clean them. This practice disrupts the production scheduling not to mention the inefficiency in high-salaried employees (cooks and their assistants) performing the work of low-priced employees (dishwashers). Also the work load for the dish room crew is not leveled out as some pots and pans are always ready for washing prior to the delivery of soiled dishes from the dining room.

Frozen food from the raw-food holding area can only be handled in one of two ways if the kitchen is to comply with sanitation standards. The food can either be thawed in a standard $34°F(1°C)$ refrigerator or cooked without thawing. The only problem in cooking frozen food stuffs will be in the cook's lack of expertise. He or she must learn two basic rules—(1) do not sear frozen meat; (2) in using ovens, cook at the lowest temperature possible. Frozen steaks should start on the low-heat side of the broiler (fresh steaks are always seared by placing them on the hottest portion to seal in the juices). It is always better, however, if the product can be refrigerator thawed. A manager must plan ahead to have the necessary time to do the thawing.

In any restaurant, perhaps the most difficult planning is for the movement of people and things. In a completely organized universe people will always provide unpredictable patterns that it is the manager's job to understand. In order to accomplish this in the food business you must have the proper equipment and personnel trained in its use. In moving materials the following must be considered:

- raw materials to the four basic areas
- raw materials within the basic areas
- finished product to the customer in the dining room
- soiled dishes to the dish room
- clean dishes to the cooks
- clean eating gear to the dining room
- garbage to the holding area

The equipment needed for this movement is as follows:

- flat-bed, four-wheel carts, 24 inches or 30 by 48 inches, with pulling and steering handle
- stainless steel three-shelf carts, 16 by 30 inches
- trays or dessert carts to move the finished dishes to the customer
- plate covers
- tray stands

The flat beds move bulk materials from raw-holding areas into the kitchen and move the garbage cans to the garbage-holding area. The stainless steel "tea carts" are for the cooks to move products (such as panned rib roasts) within the preparation area. The trays or dessert carts move the plated or prepared

A three-tiered pass-through shelf also can be used for holding ready items.

food to the customer. In transporting plates with food from kitchen to customer, they must always have plate covers on them. Trays on the carts are used to transport the soiled dishes from the dining room.

Humanscale is a term devised by Mr. Henry Dreyfuss, famous engineer and author, to indicate that designers must keep in mind that "people" use the equipment. In his book *Designing for People* (P.B. Grossman Penguin) he relates the size and shape of people to the kitchen-production equipment. This anthropometric data contains twenty thousand pieces of information to be used by the designers in considering all physical angles. At the present time it is only available to Americans as it is scaled to persons with a like physianatomy. A good designer, however, could convert the measurements for any culture.

Many kitchens contain equipment that the cooks no longer use. The changing style of merchandizing, such as precut steaks and chops, has practically eliminated the need for a meat saw. From observation, the manager can determine those items that could be removed, saving space and maintenance.

All types of refrigeration equipment from the largest walk-in to the smallest reach-in boxes can be purchased with external compressors and motors. In many instances these can be located outside the kitchen, reducing the heat and noise.

The modern kitchen must have all the labor-saving equipment possible using only space and financing as constraints. Some of these are:

- electric can openers
- blenders (commercial size)
- portion scales
- can crusher and trash compactor
- can dollies
- garbage disposal unit
- scraping and work tables
- carts
- dish trucks
- mobile steam-cleaning unit
- mop truck
- calculator
- two and three compartment sinks
- hand dryer
- electric meat slicer
- patty maker
- toaster
- tenderizer
- trunion and tilting kettles
- fat filter
- table-top mixer
- bulletin board
- guest-check holder
- microwave oven
- bun warmer
- rinse injector on dishwasher machine
- conveyor toaster

Electric fans in ovens, commonly known as convectaire,

accomplish a number of things. They eliminate oven hot-spots and speed up cooking by circulating the hot air.

Food Divison—Service Section

The dining room is the "show spot" of any club and must be designed so that it creates the desired atmosphere or theme. Some clubs create very formal, elegant appearances, others want to be more casual. The one word that is applicable to all is "nice."

If a new club was being designed the following would be considered:

- the number of members
- the number of members plus guests who would require specific food service; there are a number of variables in calculating this, some of which are type of club, location, membership economic structure, and recreation facilities.

In the physical organization of the dining rooms the first step is to determine the number and size of the tables and chairs that will be used. Normally the dining room will be set with dueces, fours, sixes, and eights. This means that the tables will be prepared and reset.

The club standard for dining is fifteen square feet per person. This is higher than the average in commercial restaurants but is needed to create the spacious atmosphere. This includes the aisle and waitress stations.

For the purposes of an example, a one-hundred-and-fifty-member dining room is used. For larger rooms use these factors and expand. Using one hundred and fifty diners and the 15 square feet (1.6 square meters) figure a minimum of 2250 square feet (207.5 square meters) would be needed.

In a club dining room that seats one hundred and fifty persons the following arrangements would work very well. Set up:

21 tables for four persons—total 84
10 tables for two persons—total 20
5 tables for six persons—total 30
2 tables for eight persons—total 16

Total 150

The tables for two and four persons can be rectangle and square and be merged to seat four, six, and eight. The tables for six and eight persons can be round. In setting up the room for banquets usually the square-foot-per-person is reduced to 12 square feet and only round tables are used, set up for eight to ten persons.

The planning should include one waiters' station for each thirty diners, and our one-hundred-and-fifty-person room would need five stations. These should contain some extra china, glasses, silverware, linen, condiments, ice water, ice, coffee maker, serving bowls, a crumber and dish, and paper towels. If at all possible running water should be available at the station.

In planning a cafeteria, the seating is usually ten square feet per person, including aisles. This can be worked into the club kitchen plan so that a multiple use is accomplished. The cafeteria line can be a waiter's pick-up station when table service is desired. It is important to plan the speed of the line to suit the dining room. With one busboy to every fifty patrons, the line should be geared to ten patrons or less every minute. One waiter station would be sufficient for the room.

Glasses. All glasses should have stems. The bulk of the glassware will be eight or more ounces for water, milk, iced tea, coffee, ades, etc. The stem separating the liquid container from the table stops condensation and makes for a neater table, eliminating the need for an underliner in some cases. If patrons will be adding anything to the beverage, such as sugar, lemon, etc., an underliner must be used.

China. The chinaware pattern should be plain but elegant, plates should have a serving lip (a space for the food server's thumb), cups should have an easily graspable handle, sugars and creamers should have lids, and saucers should not be deeply ridged. Investigate the new china with steel, aluminum and fiber-glass strands in them, if the pattern is being changed. Always plan to have some matching solid color earthenware for specialty goods. Plate covers of metal or plastic are a must.

Silverware. Silverware should have some weight to it but patterns must not be too ornate. The design must be such that the dish machine will thoroughly wash the handles. Intricate or very deep designs will trap food particles. Quality plates are used in certain dining rooms with sterling silver for special affairs.

Linen. The club uses linen in many departments and management has many options on how to provide it. These are based on quality, rental, service availability, price, laundering equipment, and club storage-space.

Regarding *quality*, the club will need fine napery for the dining rooms and very nice looking uniforms for employees. If these can be furnished by a linen rental service then the management has the option of using them or not.

The complete cost of each of the following should be figured:

- rental cost
- purchase price
- cost of laundering both by vendor and in-house
- cost of laundry equipment; if the club must purchase, what is the amortization table?

Storage space could be a determining factor. If the club purchases its own linen then the complete supply must be stored.

Management also might be able to use different methods for different items. The uniforms for kitchen and maintenance staff may not be as critical as those for waiters, waitresses, and bar persons. Therefore the manager might have a mix of owned and rented linen.

The last item to consider is the cost of paper service. In some geographical areas, club owned and laundered linen has been found to be more economical than paper.

Bar and Cocktail Lounge Division—Preparation Section

In designing the bar and cocktail lounge it is always desirable to consider whether a preparation area or service bar is necessary. A service bar is one at which only drinks are prepared for third-party service. A bartender prepares a drink, a waiter or waitress receives it and serves it to the customer. This area can be very useful and speed table service in both the dining and lounge sections of the club. In many clubs this is not part of the basic design as many designers consider a bar both a production and customer service; most are, in commercial bars and restaurants. In a club, however, drinks as a club service may be served in a

Salad bars add a nice touch to luncheon dining and are favored by many members.

number of areas in addition to those of the commercial restaurant. Drinks may be served in card, game, and locker rooms, poolside, lounge areas, etc. Efficiency as well as economy must be considered.

The manager must keep in mind that only service sells drinks at tables, whether they are in the cocktail lounge, dining room, or party room. Therefore the manager must make table service easy for the service personnel.

The points to consider are:

1. In the distance from customers' table to drink source, how many steps could be saved if a service bar was established in the pantry?
2. Is there sufficient business to warrant another bartender? If there are already two, could service be greatly improved by having one behind a service bar?
3. How does the bar drink-control-system work?
4. Could an automatic service-bar be used? (If it can be placed so that a food checker is between the bar and the customer this might work very well.)

Another use for a bar preparation area is to premix drinks and provide a ready holding area. Under Internal Revenue Regulations alcoholic beverages may be premixed and held in other than tax-stamped bottles. The time span allowed is very short but it is a tremendous time-saver for the very popular mixed drinks such as martinis and Manhattans.

Bar and Cocktail Lounge Division—Service Section

The successful bar and cocktail lounge should be planned to occupy 15 percent of the total club customer area. In computing this the dining room, party, and banquet rooms, and other customer facilities are considered. For example:

Dining room	3000 sq. ft.
Party rooms (3)	2000 sq. ft.
Billiard room	900 sq. ft.
Card room	480 sq. ft.
	6380 sq. ft.

The bar and cocktail lounge then is 15 percent of 6380 or 957 square feet.

In the lounge allow 10 square feet per customer in planning tables. Use the same percentage of sizes as in the dining room. It may also be necessary to establish a bar in locations convenient to sports areas. These might be for golfers, tennis players, etc.

A service bar may be just a table set up with bottles, glasses, garnishments, and ice, or can be built-in and have running water and a drain. The latter is called a wet bar.

In the event the manager is consulted on planning the bar the following may be useful:

1. A straight bar is much easier for the bartender to work. He can provide good service to more people than if the bar is any other shape.

2. Plan so that the bartender faces the customer as much as possible. This means he must have equipment under and over the bar. Under the bar he will need a sink, work shelf, garnishment dishes for onions, olives, cherries, oranges, slices of lime, lemon, and pineapple, mint, etc. A sink or container for ice must also be provided, if the bar does not have an undercounter ice-maker. A speedrail (a metal hanger to hold the alcoholic beverages selected as the bar stock) is needed and a pre- or post-mix water and soda dispensing system.

On the bar splashrail coasters, stirrers, and servettes may be placed. Above the bar the glasses may be stored.

3. In this setup the bartender turns from the customer only to ring up the sale. A system is being developed, however, where this will be done automatically for him. Until this system is perfected a cash register could be recessed in the bar. This would normally not be acceptable in most clubs as the drinks are charged and should be prerung. This means that some type of guest check is used and each round of drinks is recorded by the cash-register printer.

4. Plan the space between the bar and back bar (the bartenders' working space) at 2½ feet if bartenders do not cross each other, 4 feet if they do.

5. Allow 2½ feet space for each stool and always purchase stools with sturdy backs, but no sides. This will reduce bar-stool accidents. Never anchor the stools as they might have to be removed for special occasions or on busy nights.

The equipment needed in the bar and cocktail lounge is as follows:

- bar and backbar
- pre- or postmix water and soda system
- draft beer system
- sinks and drains
- icemaker
- cooler for consumer-size products
- blender
- cash register
- automatic drink-measuring systems
- speed rail
- cutting board
- knives, forks, spoons
- ice crusher
- bar stools
- cocktail tables and chairs
- glasses

Catering Division

The word "catering" is used to describe a club function specifically ordered by a club member or a group of members, planned with club personnel, paid for by the member or members, and not open to the general membership. It may be a full banquet, a meal, just food or beverages, and may be held on club property or in a member's home.

In the club business it is well to plan "room service" if the property includes a hotel/motel as part of the catering division.

Catering is a very important function of every club as it is a service that is not available in all other establishments. It can be profitable and act as an outstanding promotion device.

In the club business, the catering department is never established as part of an original organization. The catering duties are accomplished with existing personnel—until such time as the demand exceeds the resources; then a catering division is developed. This book will discuss catering as a division of the food and beverage department.

Catering is the place for the entire staff to show their professionalism. It gives management an opportunity to dress up the club and use the fine china, glassware, linen, and silverware it has saved for these occasions. One club has a complete gold service it offers to members for their use at catered affairs. Another club in Manila has complete costume changes in at least four styles for all employees who serve the special party. It gives the chef and his staff an opportunity to use their creativeness in setting menus, buffet-tables service, and other items, while offering the service staff a challenge to serve the meal properly and promptly, changing the routine of all those involved.

Catering Division—Sales Layout

The manager must plan a space for the selling of the catered affairs. This can be in the catering manager's office or a quiet place in the club. It is important that the member planning the party has the undivided attention of the club employee. The "red carpet" should really be rolled out (coffee served in the morning, a cold drink in the afternoon).

Catering Division—Service Layout

A space in the kitchen should be available to plate food and to move the mobile equipment to the serving area. The cart should be heated and connected to an outlet convenient to the plating area. These carts are now designed to hold trays as well as plates. A holding and unloading area should be established for each party or banquet room so that the cart can again be plugged in to keep the food hot until served. Refrigerated carts should also be used for the cold foods. If the kitchen and party rooms are separated horizontally or vertically by more than 150 feet then a space outside the rooms should be provided for some fixed refrigeration equipment. This speeds up service as salads, desserts, etc. can be prepared and held well before any guests arrive. This area could also be used for banquet-service gear.

Retail Sales—Layout and Design

The retail sales department includes all sales made to members other than the food and beverages sold through the kitchen or over the bar. These sales include, but are not limited to:

- all pro shop sales
- all vending-machine sales
- all rentals—lockers, clubs, rackets, or other sport gear, catering gear (always in coordination with the catering division)
- all fees and charges, with the exception of dues and assessments
- motel and/or hotel rooms

The head of this department, unless it was an assigned duty of some other department head, will need a furnished office, including an adding machine and calculator.

The layout and design of the shops should be planned by a retail-store-design expert.

Support Systems Department—Layout and Design

The support systems department will provide the club with services and will need space in which to perform them.

The head of the department will be the comptroller and an office should be provided as, in addition to supervising the staff, this person will be analyzing the financial condition of the club, reporting on cash flow, cost controls, budgeting, and other related matters.

The accounting division will need space to do the bookkeeping, record maintenance, and cost control.

The club cashier will need a private room with a locked dutch door-type of arrangement or a cage within an existing space. This space should be accessible to both members and employees with the members having priority if management must make a choice.

The receiving clerk should have a desk in the holding room for dry stores.

The support systems department will also have control of office supplies for the club. A locked room or cabinet will be needed.

Maintenance Department—Layout and Design

The maintenance department has the responsibility for keeping every item in the entire club usable and also for the club's up-keep and cleanliness. In almost all clubs the cleanliness or clean-up does not include the kitchen as this is the chef's responsibility.

The department is divided into divisions. These are determined by the size and complexity of the operation. The three main divisions usually are: janitorial, grounds maintenance, and repairs. In some clubs the same persons will perform all three functions; in others, there will be some personnel combinations; and in large clubs there may be separate personnel for each division.

The layout and design for this department is very complicated as it primarily concerns storage space for supplies and equipment in every building; as well as outside storage space. In addition the department will need a fairly well-equipped workshop.

In clubs located on former farms, barns have been kept in good condition for storage; other clubs have had to build facilities. In any climate where equipment is not used on a year-round basis it pays to protect the equipment such as trucks, tractors, mowers, etc.

As regards interior maintenance, many clubs pay dearly for poor planning by not being able to use cleaning machines for rugs, mosaics, and tiles because of lack of storage space.

The maintenance department should have an office, a tool and stock room, and a workshop. These can be located together in or around the main clubhouse, or can be housed in other buildings.

Recreational Facilities—Layout and Design

It is customary for a club to hire professionals to design the recreational facilities but this should be limited to things the players use. Too often knowledgeable course, court, and pool designers get involved in designing service areas such as shops, restaurants, and kitchens that result in management nightmares.

The designer of the golf course may or may not be qualified to design the pro shop. If management is involved in planning, check the designer's qualifications. The following questions should be considered in providing advice and guidance to the experts:

1. Are there any combinations possible? Can the new tennis courts be located so that the golf locker room can be used, or the snack bars?
2. If an informal cocktail lounge is needed, can it service more than one sport group?
3. Is parking possible so that sports and main club facilities can be used without moving cars?
4. Can every facility be designed within one building to save labor, supplies, energy, and security costs?
5. Are spectator spaces provided for the recreation facilities?
6. Can a handicapped person view the action?
7. Will lighting the areas for night activities now or later present a major problem?
8. Is storage space provided for club-owned seasonal property?
9. Have wind and sun factors been considered in layout and design?
10. Is the entrance to the sauna, baths, or steam rooms convenient for both women and men?

REVIEW QUESTIONS

1. The number of departments a club has is determined by what factors?
2. What are the advantages of departmentalization from a management standpoint?
3. Under what circumstances might a manager get an opportunity to advise on layout and design?
4. Are there specific areas that the manager may be able to correct with minor renovation?
5. Discuss the effect of "human scale" on the design and placement of equipment.

6. Discuss the rationale for emphasizing the catering aspect of the club business.

7. Discuss the ways a manager should get involved in renovations in the recreational areas.

8. Given the following data determine the square footage of a kitchen to service these facilities.

> 2500 sq. ft. of dining room
> 1800 sq. ft. of party rooms
> 500 sq. ft. of snack bar

9. A large room in the club has dividers to partition it in 1000 square foot segments. How many segments would be used to set up dining table service for one setting of 270 members?

10. Without reservations from the members, and without any prior sales experience figures, list the number of dueces, sixes, and eights you would set up for the 270 persons?

11. How many service stations would be established?

4

Personnel

Management

OVERVIEW

This chapter will detail and analyze the complexities of personnel management in the form of a filled-out reference outline. Personnel problems with causes, effects, and suggested solutions are pictured.

By personnel simplification, this chapter will give the manager a working knowledge and confidence in interviewing, hiring, training, and developing employees. Also the manager will learn how to delegate part of the management responsibilities and authority to the club subordinate supervisors.

THE BUSINESS OF PEOPLE

The club business is the ultimate people business. The lifeblood of the club is the membership and the manager deals with them through the employees. The effectiveness of the manager's talent in dealing with people is his performance benchmark. This chapter will deal with the club employees.

For operating personnel, the club business is by far more stable than its hospitality counterparts. This relates to the caliber of the employees, in terms of loyalty and turnover. Clubs are far advanced in the field of salaries and employee benefits in comparison with most of the hotel and restaurant industry. The manager's objectives with the club employee are:

- respect for manager leadership
- productivity
- courtesy and service to the members

The manager needs the respect of his employees in order to communicate with them effectively. This communication may be an order, an instruction, a question, or a reprimand; but it carries its proper weight only when the employee listens and responds. This cannot be wholly successful without respect because the employee, viewing the manager as an individual, receives communications with different emotions. If the employee respects the manager, knowing he is honest, knowledgeable, circumspect, and fair, then the manager may know that his performance will be effective.

The manager earns the employee's respect in the following ways:

1. *By being honest*; the manager does not lie or cheat, and does not do anything in the club that would appear to be lying or cheating. Examples of these types of actions are:

   - cashing a postdated check
   - borrowing from the club; this could be either in cash or goods
   - lying to a club officer or employee
   - no recording of merchandise used

2. *By being knowledgeable*; the manager must not only know the business but must convince the employees that he does.

3. *By being circumspect in behavior*; the manager cannot drink at the bar, be sloppy in dress or conduct and expect to gain respect. The manager sets the behavior pattern for the club.

4. *By being fair*; the manager must see that all employees are treated the same and receive equal pay for equal work.

5. *By not socializing* with the employees.

In order to manage a club successfully, if there are problems, management must know their reasons and solutions. Therefore this chapter deals with problems that are caused by people. (In later chapters, problems that are caused by materials will be discussed.)

To know the club, management will have to observe every facet of its operation. The manager must learn to view the club not only as a manager but as a member, remembering that the member is paying for the club privileges.

ORGANIZING CLUB PERSONNEL

The organizing of the club personnel is very simple if management is starting from scratch with no employees. This might be the situation at a new club or one that is reopening. Unfortunately this is a rare situation few managers will ever get a chance to experience. The average problem that faces a manager is provided by the "inherited" organization. The major personnel problems that beset most clubs can be directly attributed to internal organization. These problems are usually poor food and drinks, poor service, poor maintenance, and discontented employees. These can sometimes be caused by:

- departments and divisions not being clearly defined; each employee must know that he has a supervisor whom he must please to continue his/her employment
- salary scale equated to longevity; an excellent example of this is having an employee with a menial job making more money than a skilled cook only because he has been on the same job for "twenty-plus years"
- personality and good work; this person is pleasant, cheerful, and a good worker but has no ambition to be promoted and consequently has been given raises indiscriminately so that now the salary is beyond that usually paid for the job

- favoritism and nepotism; this employee has been unfairly favored by the management and/or the members and is paid more than the job deserves

- no job descriptions for the positions, or none that have been put in writing, clearly defined and enforced; in some clubs employees have difficulty determining just who their supervisor is when everyone from the manager down is giving orders; or even worse is having a talented and aggressive employee step into the supervisory vacuum and assume an unauthorized position. Organizations have been torn apart:

a. by a very knowledgeable bookkeeper giving instructions to operating personnel

b. by aggressive dining-room-service personnel who have disrupted the productivity of a kitchen by exceeding their authority

c. by cocktail-service personnel creating a most unpleasant atmosphere in the lounge by challenging the authority of the bartender

d. by supervisors not having their authority defined by an organization chart showing how employees function in their departments.

These problems may be dealt with in two ways: first preventing them and second, if they are inherited, correcting them. All organization must be based on need. Department establishment and supervision is determined by economics alone, based entirely on whether the members will pay for the services presented, directly or through dues and assessments.

Thus the steps that management can take to organize the club employees are as follows:

1. Analyze the club personnel's reimbursement for the responsibility he/she has for getting a particular job done.

2. Establish a numerical chart listing the reimbursement and responsibilities.

3. Grade the jobs.

4. Establish salaries for each grade.

5. Using the methods described, work to bring the staff salaries in line with the responsibilities they have.

ANALYZING CLUB PERSONNEL

The manager will analyze the internal structure first by drawing up an organization chart. The appropriate blocks in the organization chart are now filled in with the position title and employees names. Vacancies are listed on the chart. Where an employee works for more than one department, a number is used after his or her name as an indication. For example, if Clarence Williams works as both a janitor and a dishwasher, he would be listed in the maintenance department as C. Williams (1) and in the food department as C. Williams (2).

This accomplishes the following:

1. The department, division, and section in which each employee works is detailed.
2. It pinpoints the supervisor who should be giving this employee supervision.
3. Weaknesses in the organization echelon may be more easily spotted. Unusual structures will have been revealed by this method, giving guidelines for corrective measures.

NUMBERING EMPLOYEES

One method of keeping accurate records of labor costs is to give each department, division, or section a letter starting with "A." The unit then becomes a "cost center" and not only labor but all expenses can be tracked to it. The individual employees are designated in the books of the club by their social security numbers. For example, using the social security numbers of each employee, add a letter after the nine-digit number to indicate the department in which the employee worked. Food and beverage department has twenty full-time and forty part-time employees. The letter for this department could be A. Recreation has eight full-time and twenty-five part-time; the letter could be B. Retail Sales has seven full-time and two part-time; the letter could be C. Support Systems has six full-time and one part-time; the letter could be D. Maintenance has eleven full-time and thirty part-time; the letter could be E.

REIMBURSEMENT AND RESPONSIBILITY CHARTS

Management must have a method to study the overall personnel structure of the club and one vehicle that can be used is a *Reimbursement and Responsibility Chart.*

Table 4-1. Reimbursement and Responsibility Chart

Employees	Management Responsibility	Salary
Manager	1	
Assistant Manager	2	
Night Manager	3	
Food and Beverage Manager	4	5
Recreation Manager	5	8
Retail Sales Manager	6	11
Comptroller	7	4
Maintenance Department Manager	8	12
Chef	9	3
Golf Professional	10	1
Tennis Professional	11	2
Bar Manager	12	15
Catering Division Manager	13	14
Purchasing Agent	14	17
Ground Maintenance Foreman	15	6
Hotel Manager	16	16
Bookkeeper	17	7
Maitre d'Hotel	18	9
Dining Room Hostess	19	18
Head Cashier	20	20
Head Janitor	21	10
Senior Life Guard	22	19
Dish and Ware Washing Supervisor	23	13

To prepare this chart the manager would start by listing each supervisory position in the club in order of importance. For example in the management ladder the manager would be number 1, with subordinate positions following in their order of importance. This of course will be the manager's opinion but his judgement must prevail. Next, the salary paid for each position is listed with the highest salary paid indicated by the number 1. Then the rest of the salaries are given numbers (the higher the salary the lower the number).

Compilation of the chart is the first step; but is must be put aside until a wage scale for superivosrs can be compiled.

Now management is ready to develop a *Reinbursement and Responsibility Chart* for each cost center. One is shown here.

Employees by Cost Center
Food and Beverage—A

Social Security Number + A	Name	Position	Rank by Salary	Rank by Job
	Perlito	Fry Cook	1	3
	Jones	First Cook	2	1
	Peters	Pantry Person	3	6
	Alberts	Second Cook	4	5
	Troy	Sous Chef	5	2
	Simmons	Second Cook	6	7
	Mendes	Ware Washer	7	10
	Corcina	Ware Washer	8	11
	Balato	Kitchen Helper	9	8
	Pinalti	Cooks' Helper	10	9
	Jalko	Baker	11	4

A chart similar to this should be prepared showing each person in the organization as they are assigned to a department. Once these charts are completed then a complete organization chart can be established.

Analyzing the *Reimbursement and Responsibility Charts,* it

is apparent that management positions will need a careful study as they do not seem organizationally acceptable—the reimbursement responsibilities are not matched in all positions. The following are areas that should be studied on the first chart:

Recreation manager	8th on scale
Retail sales manager	11th on scale
Tennis pro	2nd on scale
Bar manager	15th on scale
Catering department manager	14th on scale
Purchasing agent	17th on scale
Bookkeeper	7th on scale
Head janitor	10th on scale
Dish and Ware Washing supervisor	13th on scale

The areas on the second chart are:

Warewashers	7th and 8th on scale
Baker	11th on scale

These charts now have indicated the areas that need management attention and perhaps correction. The "perhaps" in corrections means there may be unusual circumstances that will make the manager revise the responsibility column of the chart.

In the event the manager's first estimate of reimbursement and responsibilities is correct then action must be taken. The actions management takes to correct these discrepancies will effect the morale not only of the employees concerned, but all club employees. Therefore all details of the problem must be carefully considered before any action may be taken.

DEFINED DEPARTMENTS

Using the information that has been developed, the manager can try to departmentalize the club properly. This means that each department, division, and section will have a supervisor.

The supervisor will know the employees he or she is responsible for and what jobs they should be doing.

One basic concept of management that cannot be ignored is that each employee must have only one boss at one time. An employee may have more than one boss—but not during the same time period. For example, four janitors are needed at 8 A.M. to prepare the club for business; but by noon only one person is needed. During this time they work for, and are supervised by, the head janitor; after lunch, however, three of these employees will work for grounds maintenance. The supervisors understand this structure as do the employees—therefore no confusion.

WAGE SCALES

The first step in management's corrective action is to study the existing wage scales in the club, and establishing them if they are nonexistent. The basic management policy is to reimburse all workers on the premise that equal work equates with equal pay.

A wage scale will first be divided by separating the management employees from all the others. Management employees are listed, then graded by hourly or annual rates, since members of the management team may be paid in either of these ways. But the supervisors of those employees doing semiskilled tasks (such as head janitor, or head dishwasher) are usually scaled on an hourly rate. The establishment or rate type has no bearing on whether the supervisor is a working manager or not.

Supervisors who are on an hourly rate receive 50 cents per hour above the highest rate paid for the worker and participate in the annual rate increases along with the employees.

The term per annum or annual rate applies to a position where a flat salary is paid regardless of the hours worked. This salary is subject to all state laws and in some instances federal laws as well.

After the employees have been separated into the two wage-scale groups then a position description should be prepared for each employee as follows, listing:

1. Job title and summary of duties
2. Typical work performed with the percent of time spent on each task
3. Nature of supervisory responsibility
   - planning
   - work direction
   - administration
   - responsibility
   - who the employee reports to
4. Level and complexity of work supervised
   - identification of subordinate positions by job name
   - identification of elements over which the position has only administrative supervision
   - identification of specific complexities such as fluctuating sales
   - size of work force supervised
   - qualifications required for this position.

Now the manager checks these job descriptions against his *Reimbursement and Responsibilities Chart* and makes whatever adjustments are necessary.

The salary scale for all employees should have built-in longevity increases for satisfactory service.

All salaries should have a range from low to high of twelve increments. The salary paid to the junior executive should begin the wage scale, with each executive level of responsibility advancing three steps. Using 5 percent as the increment increase the scale would look as follows (see Exhibit 4–1). It is noted that the manager and assistant manager are not listed under the salary in the *Reimbursement and Responsibility Chart* (Table 4–1), the reason being that these salaries have very little relationship to the others. A good assistant manager might make up to 50 percent of the manager's salary, a good night manager up to 40 percent.

The manager will now establish the two wage scales for his club. The executive scale (Exhibit 4–1) starts with the minimum salary for executives as set by the Fair Labor Standards Act (federal law) because an executive may work the number of

Exhibit 4-1. Executive Salary Scale

Grade	1st Step	2nd Step	3rd Step	4th Step	5th Step	6th Step
1	8000	8400	8820	9261	9724	10,213
2	9261	9724	10,212	10,723	11,259	11,821
3	10,723	11,259	11,821	12,412	13,032	13,683

Grade	7th Step	8th Step	9th Step	10th Step	11th Step	12th Step
1	10,723	11,259	11,821	12,412	13,032	13,032
2	12,412	13,032	13,683	14,367	15,085	15,839
3	14,367	15,085	15,839	16,630	17,461	18.334

hours that it takes to get the job done, and receive no overtime. The worker's scale (Exhibit 4-2) starts with the state or federal (whichever is the highest) minimum wage. The minimum wage does not apply to clubs with a gross business of

less than 275,000 dollars now
less than 325,000 dollars as of 1 July 1980
less than 362,500 dollars as of 1981

In establishing the minimum wage, tipped employees may also be considered. The federal law allows a 45 percent reduction in the hourly rate paid an employee if the employee will receive this amount in tips. This changes to 40 percent in 1980 and will be abolished 1 January 1981. However there are states

Exhibit 4-2. Worker's Salary Scale

Grade	1st Step	2nd Step	3rd Step	4th Step	5th Step	6th Step	7th Step	8th Step	9th Step	10th Step	11th Step	12th Step
1	2.65	2.79	2.93	3.08	3.23	3.39	3.55	3.73	3.92	4.12	4.33	4.55
2	3.08	3.23	3.39	3.55	3.73	3.92	4.12	4.33	4.55	4.78	5.02	5.27

that also have laws on tip credit, and these prevail. For example, the state of California does not allow tip credits.

The manager may also consider bonuses as part of the wage scale. These are not used as profit incentives in the same direct way as in hotels and restaurants, but are used to stimulate achieving percentage goals.

The only worthwhile bonus is one in which the club benefits. Christmas and other bonuses must be tied to attendance, performance, visible courtesy, or other club-related objectives in order to be of any value. If management is trapped into a type of bonus that provides no club benefits it should be changed to a constructive one as rapidly as possible.

Bonuses can be based on membership count, customer count, sales and percentage goals. Percentage goals for management personnel, however, are the most beneficial to the club. For example if management decides that the club should operate with a 30-percent food cost when up to 35 percent will be acceptable, then, if the actual cost is 31 percent, the food department head gets 4 percent for himself or to split with his employees after labor costs. Bonuses should never be easy to achieve and must be of value to the club.

It is also a good idea to allow the department head to control the bonus completely. Bonuses are taxable—thus management can monitor the bonus distribution.

Grading the positions in accordance with responsibilities does not mean that every position would have a different grade. Many clubs have found that various positions carry similar responsibilities, thus salaries are the same. One club with twelve executives, using this chart, needed five grades.

The chart (Exhibit 4–2) for hourly workers is the same using the lowest hourly rate paid and setting up an increment scale of 5 percent.

The manager grades the positions using the *Reimbursement and Responsibility Charts* and then analyzes the pay. The following indicates the various broad reimbursement and responsibility equations that the manager may use. The positions are listed in order of importance.

8. Chef-Golf professional
7. Heads of support systems, and retail sales department

6. Bar manager, catering manager, tennis professional, baker

5. Purchasing agent, grounds maintenance foreman, hotel manager, maitre d'hotel, first cook, sous chef, garde manager, and bartender

4. Bookkeeper, butcher, head janitor, social director, and second cook

3. Head cashier, senior life guard, head waitress

2. Dish and ware washing supervisor, hostess, clerks, and drivers

1. Waiters, waitresses, janitors, helpers, buspersons, lifeguards, and dishwashers

These eight classifications by job importance now may be matched against wage scales to set job salaries.

Longevity policy is established then as follows:

- 52 calendar weeks of satisfactory service in grade 1 to go to steps 2, 3, and 4
- 104 calendar weeks of satisfactory service in grade 4 to go to steps 5, 6, and 7
- 156 calendar weeks of satisfactory service in grade 7 to go to steps 8. 9, and 10
- 260 calendar weeks of satisfactory service in grade 10 to go to steps 11 and 12

This policy is purposely lengthy and charts a particular job for twenty-nine years. It is done to encourage the employees to increase their skills by outside or in-house training so that they can be promoted as openings become available.

PROMOTION: PERFORMANCE, POLITICS, AND THE WAGE SCALE

Payment of employees for more than the job is worth must be investigated and corrected. As management created this problem, only good management can correct it. Some of the ways that this is corrected are:

1. Consult with the employee, show the wage scale and explain that the jobs are all graded. Indicate on the scale the employee's job and the top and bottom hourly rates of the scale. The wages being

above the high for the grade, locate on the scale the positions that can meet this amount. For example, if the employees job was in grade 1 and the stipend was $4.12 per hour explain that he must train for a job in grades 2 or 3 if he wishes to retain this salary. A training program is established and the employee is given a reasonable time to qualify. After learning the skills for the new position of say, bartender, the employee retains the $4.12 per hour until there is an opening and then the promotion is made. The pay is also raised to the next increment as a reward for the employee's cooperation. If this policy is established and the employee is not agreeable to training, then the wages paid should be reduced to the top in the grade.

2. Create a new supervisor position and promote the employee into it. For example, one dishwasher is making a higher hourly wage than the other dishwashers and above the highest paid for the job at $4.55 per hour. This is an excellent employee and perhaps the dish room could use some supervision, or the employee may actually be the supervisor without the title. If the next-highest-paid dishwasher is earning wages within grade 1 then $4.55 will be at least 50 cents per hour more and this works out well.

3. Arbitrarily reduce the employee's hourly rate. This could have a serious effect on morale but many conglomerates on taking over have done this.

4. Release the employee. This also could be hard on morale but is based on the theory that no one gives top performance in a job for an indefinite period.

Management must understand that if no action is taken the situation will further deteriorate if employees get cost-of-living raises or bonuses.

Fringe Benefits

Fringe benefits are those goods, services, etc. that an employee is given in addition to salary. Some of the usual ones in the club business are insurance, vacation and other types of paid leave, meals, lodging, transportation, discounts, use of facilities, education, stock options, entertainments, expenses, social security, workmen's compensation, and unemployment insurance.

The manager divides these benefits into four categories,

those he can control, those he cannot control, those reserved for management, and those imposed on him by law. It is very difficult to have any hard and fast rules regarding fringe benefits because of the location of the club, its financial condition, its age, and the social attitude of its members. The following, however, will make management aware of the costly problems fringe benefits can cause.

Controllable Benefits

These are fringe benefits that the manager controls and are never given arbitrarily. There must be a reason for each benefit and they are only packaged as necessary. Divided into two groups, they are one, available to all employees, and two, are given to selected individuals. The benefits for all employees could be the following:

Retirement Insurance—Management should plan to pay a generous share, at least 50 percent, of the cost of retirement insurance. Insurance should be mandatory (if the employee works for the club he must take the insurance) and the employee may retire or be retired by the club at age fifty-five after ten years of satisfactory service. This, while seeming very generous, gives management tight control over nonproductive older employees.

Leave—Each club can have four types of leave. *Annual leave*—this is used by the employee for vacation or personal needs. The employee must request and management can grant or not in accordance with need. A sound cumulative policy is two hours leave for each week worked in grades 1 to 5 and 3 hours each week for employees in grades 6, 7, and 8. Executives in grades 1 to 3 would receive 3 hours each week, those in 4 and above 4 hours. As this is taken as a weekly payroll expense and set up as a working reserve, the employee may accumulate (without limit) and will be paid upon leaving the club's employment whether it is voluntary, involuntary, retirement, or death. The accumulation of leave is a right, the granting of the leave is a privilege controlled by management. *Sick leave*—this is to be used by an employee for personal illness only. The employee must request it and management can grant or not grant sick leave. A policy should be established that if an employee is out over three days, management can require a doctor's certificate before the employee is paid sick leave. The accumulation for all employees should be the same, two hours per week. The employee may accumulate sick leave without limit, but will only be paid for unused leave at retirement or death. No reserve is established. The accumulation of this leave is a right, the granting of it is a privilege. *Administrative leave*—this leave is reserved for the manager's discretion. The manager is the only person who can grant it and it can be used for any purpose. For example, an outstanding employee is ill and has used all his sick and annual leave and it appears the employee is on the mend and will return. The manager can keep the employee on the payroll with "administrative leave." *Leave without pay*—this can be used as punishment for wrong-doing or as a means to keep an employee on the club rolls. For example, an employee, who is otherwise satisfactory, is habitually late, sometimes causing the management embarrassment. The employee may be given days off without pay as punishment. A uniform scale of "crime and punishment" is not recommended as these matters are best left to the manger's discretion.

Meals—Until just a few years ago all eating establishments furnished their employees meals. The wages were very low, employees were often transient, and feeding them was considered necessary. Today, many clubs do not furnish free meals to employees but require them to purchase meals at a small discount. Any charge for meals is highly recommended and a regular guest-check system can be used for control. The employee prepares a guest check, blanks are kept by the chef, and the value of the meal is deducted from the employees pay. If free meals are furnished, a record must also be maintained as the value of the meal is considered pay for FICA purposes.

Lodging—This is frequently necessary in remote areas but may still be considered a fringe benefit. Usually furnished without charge, it is nevertheless considered pay for FICA purposes.

Discounts—Employees are frequently offered a discount when they purchase merchandise at a club shop. Such purchases are nontaxable.

Education—Good management is interested in all employees improving themselves. Training either in- or out-of-house pays more dividends to the club than any other type of benefit. Management can have an educational plan to train employees so that many of them are able to perform more than one job competently. The club can pay for this with tuitions and/or wages. Tuition payments made by the club for an employee are not taxable.

Uncontrollable Benefits

Benefits that management cannot control offer little or no support to the club. They are strictly sociological in nature and should be carefully studied before implementation. It is much more profitable to the club to pay for benefits in cash, letting the employee decide whether or not he wants them. Typical uncontrollable benefits are:

- hospitalization insurance
- group life insurance
- disability and/or accident insurance

For example, rather than administer hospitalizaton insurance itself, the club should solicit a good company, turn over the employees' names, and request the company to make direct contacts. The average cost of the insurance (the rates differ for persons who are single, married, have families, etc.) are then added to the employee's pay check as an increase in the hourly or per-annum rate. A year of 40-hour weeks is 2080 hours, or 173.33 hours per month. The average monthly premium is divided by 173.33 to determine the additional hourly rate. This can be reduced if the club pays a percentage of the rate and the employee pays his/her part. It does not matter whether the employee purchases insurance or not—he gets the increased rate. This method of sharing premium payment is fair. In many companies that contribute toward employees' insurance, the insurance being voluntary, if the employee does not take the insurance he or she loses the money.

To sum up, if the club decides to purchase these types of insurance for its employees, the employees' salary should not be increased at the same time.

Some of the fringe benefits normally reserved for management are:

1. Transportation—Many clubs furnish the manager with an auto-mobile for his exclusive use. This is nontaxable if used primarily for club business.
2. Use of facilities—Most clubs will allow the manager and his family to use the facilities without charge. This is considered "close inspection" and is not taxable.
3. Education—In addition to the training available to other employees, the manager is usually encouraged to join professional organizations such as CMAA and International Military Clubs Executive Association. The club pays for dues, education meetings, and the annual trip to the Association's national conference. These fringe benefits are nontaxable.
4. Stock options—Commercial clubs sometimes give the manager stock options or stock warranties as a supplement to salary.
5. Expenses—Managers are customarily allowed to charge items to promote good will. The manager may have a set amount per month for this purpose. For example:

   • a bottle of champagne or wine sent to a table celebrating a birthday, wedding, anniversary, etc.
   • a round of drinks to soothe a justifiably irate club member
   • refreshment for a committee
   • household, living, travel, and other expenses furnished; regular meals and lodging are subject to FICA Taxes

6. Benefits imposed by law—These are the employee's share of Social Security (FICA), Workman's Compensation Insurance, and Federal and State Unemployment Insurance. While these are required by law they are still a large payroll expense and, as they are all for the employee's benefit, must be considered fringe. (The reason they are in this text is to impress on both management and employees that benefits imposed by law add a substantial cost to the payroll that is not always realized. In Florida, for example, they now add 14½ percent to the gross payroll.)

Overtime

In accordance with federal and state law, overtime must be paid to nonexecutive employees after they work a certain number of hours—if the establishment does a sufficient volume of business. The overtime rate is one-and-a-half times the regular hourly rate. The law divides these employees into two categories for the hospitality industry: (1) those employees involved in food and drink who work the first forty-four hours at regular pay and (2) all others. Membership and all dues-paying clubs are, however, not included in the food and beverage exemption and must pay overtime after 40 hours. Management always considers the job and rate so that regular employees are not paid the overtime rate if temporary employees are available. It should be noted that food-and-drink employees of profit-oriented clubs only, from 1 July 1978 on, will be paid overtime after 44 hours until 1 July 1980. After 1 July 1980, these employees and all others will be paid overtime after 40 hours.

UNIFORMS

A uniformed club staff is a must. While costly, every employee should be in management-selected outfits. Not only do uniforms save employees' clothes, but they immediately identify employees to members and employees by department. And, if selected properly, they give a touch of class to the club. On the other hand, management must help create a sense of pride in the employee wearing the uniform and develop an "esprit de corps" to give the employee a feeling of belonging. These results are easier to achieve if club members also have respect and pride in the club. Their pride creates the first incentive for pride in the employee.

Uniforms can be handled in one of two ways.

1. Purchase and give them to the employees. It is usual to give the employees three changes. The manager can pay for the laundering or dry-cleaning by cash, add it to the hourly rate, or require the employees to pay for the upkeep unless they are making only minimum wage. While washing the table and room linen at the club, the manager may also wish to clean the uniforms without charge.

2. Rent the uniforms from a uniform-rental company at the club's expense. This is the recommended procedure and this service is available from many companies. The uniforms must be new and of a design and quality specified by management.

STAFFING

The club always staffs according to need not space available. Combination jobs are the rule rather than the exception. Management always strives to keep the total numbers of employees down, using temporary employees whenever possible.

Hours of operation of all facilities are set by the board of directors, or the standing committees, at the suggestion of the manager. In staffing a facility, management should try to organize the hours of operation so that one person can do two or more jobs. Examples:

1. A cashier on the cafeteria line is only needed from 11:30 A.M. to 1:30 P.M. Perhaps the file clerk could be trained for this job also.
2. Open the dining rooms so that one eight hour shift covers them.
3. Consider creating an "on-call" service, as making drinks available on the patio to members who will "buzz" the main bar.

INTERVIEWING AND SELECTING EMPLOYEES

The Civil Rights Act of 1964, Title VII, applies to all clubs employing fifteen persons or more. Our text deals only with clubs that fall into this category.

The act bans all discrimination in employment due to race, color, religion, sex, or national origin. In addition a club manager must know about the Equal Pay Act of 1963, which bans pay discrimination for equal work because of sex; and the Age Discrimination in Employment Act of 1964, which bans discrimination because of age for anyone at least forty years old but less than sixty-five.

The interview for new employees, both oral and written, must also confirm to the Equal Employment Opportunity

The Club manager delegates the hiring of employees to the department head and his or her assistants.

guide lines. They list questions considered discriminatory such as points concerning:

- arrest and conviction records
- credit references
- contraceptive usage
- plans to have children
- unwed motherhood
- age
- height and weight
- education, unless the job really requires a certain type or amount

The interview process has only one purpose: acquire information that assists selection. It should be both oral and written. The written interview is known as the job application; the oral interview is job selection. Good selection is accomplished when the job and the applicant are matched. It has been insured that the applicant can perform the work and that the applicant will find the work satisfactory in accordance with his desires, ability, experience, and energy.

Meanwhile, the interviewer should know every qualification that is needed for the job. That includes education, emotional, physical, experience, licensing, and appearance needs. Equate the exact appearance needs with the job. Many managers have a "mirror" complex and believe every employee must act and dress as they do. They have set false standards for the job, which have no bearing on the qualifications needed. This "mirror" complex can have devastating results. Because of it, over-qualified persons are often employed for semiskilled positions. The jobs they fill do not provide an adequate challenge and the employee is soon bored and becomes a disgruntled employee lost to the club. Know in advance the type of person that is needed. Finally, have a positive recruitment plan and execute it. If part-time labor is required consider college or university placement departments. Few clubs take advantage of this source. The best time to use this plan is when you are not filling a particular position but are establishing a backlog of personnel.

CLUB POLICY

The policies relating to employees should be as few as absolutely necessary and compiled into an "orientation" book. There should be a uniform policy on conduct which should be kept broad enough to be all-inclusive. A statement such as "employee's will conduct themselves at all times like ladies and gentlemen" should cover it all. Uniform policy should be established concerning service to members, spelled out as an employee's most important function.

SAFETY

The manager is responsible for the safety of all employees. This means that the club must enforce safe working practices and conditions. The club is bound by the Occupational Safety

A menu discussion is held with the staff prior to opening the Club
Dining Room.

and Health Act (OSHA). An establishment can be heavily fined
for having unsafe working conditions. Most accidents in a club
are due to falls caused by the lack of sanitary and maintenance
standards. The primary causes are spilled foods and other
materials not being cleaned up immediately, as well as worn
spots in floors and loose stair-covering materials. The primary causes are spilled foods and other
Falls are also caused by not having the proper kinds of
ladders for the job or not insisting that the employee use the
right ladder.

SANITATION

This subject pertains only to personal sanitation in that good
grooming and good habits in employees enhances the club
image. The appearance of the employees must be the manager's
first concern. Fancy uniforms cannot cover up unkempt hair,
dirty nails, panty-hose runs, and unpolished shoes. This is where
"pride" makes its biggest contribution to management. If the

employee is proud of his job it will show in his/her appearance. It is important that this sense of pride is fostered at all times.

A human hair served to a member in his food can spoil the manager's whole day. Extra care must be taken with male employees so that if they wear their hair long, on face or head, they wear snoods while working in the food-preparation area. Management can insist that personnel meeting the public dress and act in accordance with members' expectations.

TRAINING

The training of club employees is probably the single most difficult task a manager has to perform. Training is normally needed in all departments but the manager must establish priorities. At the top of the list should be those jobs that provide service to members. The manager should concentrate on the club receptionist, food service personnel, and bartenders first. Then attention might be given:

- golf starters
- buspersons
- kitchen preparation employees
- all sales personnel
- any person who answers the telephone
- central cashier
- janitors
- maintenance men/women
- all other employees

For those categories of employees who meet, greet, or directly serve the members the training must be in two parts:

1. normal business courtesy
2. job technology

Courtesy. The first step in courtesy training is teaching the invaluable art of *recognition*. In the club business, normal business

A cheerful, courteous hostess at the *19th Hole* puts the Club members in a relaxed mood.

courtesy is different from that of a public establishment in that club members not only wish to be recognized but believe they should be. Thus the start of this training should be identification of the club officers. If the manager does not have pictures of them this should be corrected as soon as possible. The manager, who has memorized the names, will carry untitled pictures in a folder as the morning inspections are held and show unlabeled pictures to employees as he meets them. Prior to this a board is installed above the time clock with every officer's picture on it. Name and office held are under each picture.

Remembering names is habit forming. As the employees start to know the names of the officers, other members' names will become known. If the member has a title the manager must ascertain in advance whether or not the member wants it used. The goal is to call every member by their last name preceded by Mr., Mrs., Miss, or Ms., whichever is appropriate. This greeting is appropriate regardless of age. Adult males should receive an affirmative or negative reply followed by "sir;" in replying to ladies, follow the answer with her last name preceded by the appropriate form of address.

Every club employee must be taught to give all members their undivided *attention*. Every employee must know what to answer when a member questions them. If they can help, they should do so immediately, but the answer should at least be "I don't know but I will find out right away" and the employee should then know who to consult. An alert manager may even teach the janitorial and maintenance staff the answers to common questions, such as

- Is the club open today?
- What time does the bar/dining room/cocktail lounge/office/cashier/ etc. open?
- Where can I find the manager?

Members should be greeted in both the dining room and the cocktail lounge and escorted to a seat. The host/hostess should introduce the service personnel to the member, also mentioning personnel who are absent. If the member's name is known then it could be "Mr. Dugan this is Shirley/George who is your waitress/waiter" or "Mr. Dugan your waiter/waitress will be George/Shirley." The host/hostess will inform Shirley/George immediately that a table for which they are responsible is now occupied. The service employee gives the member attention, service if possible, but always attention! Attention is 50 percent of all service, setting the mood for service to come. A simple greeting usually suffices.

If introduced:

May I get you a cocktail or a carafe of wine?
Our luncheon special today is _____ .
We are featuring crown roast of lamb this evening.

If waiting on other customers, the employee breaks away as soon as possible and greets the newcomers with:

I am Shirley, your waitress this evening. I will be with you in about three minutes.

Teach employees to state a definite time and stick to it. This approach to courtesy has many advantages and provides the individualized personal attention that the members expect.

Job Technology. The manager's basic goal in training employees is the development of people. In almost every case the potential is there but some training is usually necessary. The concept of training for greater responsibilities and higher pay starts as follows:

1. the employee knows what he/she is expected to do
2. the employee has the knowledge necessary to do the task
3. the employee does the task
4. the employee then starts to receive training to increase his/her skills for a higher-grade position.

For example, the janitor is fully aware of what must be done on a daily basis. The knowledge and skills necessary to clean the floors and the daily titivation are clearly understood and he does his job. Now management must work to increase his skills so that he starts training for the next grade of positions. These jobs could be waiter, bartender, sales clerk, etc., giving management the "bench depth" that is so often lacking in the club business.

Standard Brands Sales Company back in the '50s devised an in-house training plan, the concept of which has never been improved on:

1. Before training—
   - prepare a training plan
   - prepare a job breakdown
   - have everything ready
2. When training—
   - prepare the employee for instruction:
     put the employee at ease
     explain the job and its importance
     create interest
   - present the job
   - show and tell:
     follow the job breakdowns
     explain and demonstrate one step at a time
     stress the key points
     don't tell them too much at one time

use simple language

don't do all the talking

set a high standard

give reasons for methods and procedures

show one thing at a time

give everything you want, but stop there

3. Tryout performance—
   - have the employee tell the why and the how of the job
   - make sure the employee can stress the key points
   - correct errors and omissions as they are made
   - keep in mind:

     no criticism

     let the trainees correct themselves

     don't overdo correcting

     don't correct in front of others

     don't be too quick to blame the trainee
   - encourage the trainee
   - get back everything that was given; this stage of feedback is crucial
   - continue until the trainer knows the trainee knows

4. Follow through—
   - put the employee on his/her own job
   - encourage questions from trainee and be sympathetic to all questions
   - check frequently
   - let the employee know how he/she is doing
   - have the employee do the job in the trainer's presence

ORIENTATION OF EMPLOYEES

To orient a new employee is to help the man or woman "get their bearings," help them find out where they are, what they are supposed to do and where they are going.

In orienting the new employee, management thinking should be divided into two categories, physical orientation and mental orientation. The best way to present these to an employee is (1) to have orientation materials printed in a small, neat, pocket-size booklet that the employee can keep on his/or person until all the details are known, then (2) present every detail orally and give the employee an opportunity to ask questions.

One method of doing this is to hire employees, provide them with the orientation book, then process them the following day. This gives the employee time to look over the book and perhaps ask questions during the processing period.

In a step by step process the manager should do the following.

Physical Orientation.   In the physical orientation the employee will learn:

When to report to work
Where to report to work
What to wear to work
How to get to work
Where to park a car
How to enter and leave the building
Who is their immediate superior and where they will find him/her
Where to find the time clock
How to check in and out
Where to pick up uniforms and what color they will be
Where the lockers and rest rooms are
What forms are required for the employee's signature for payroll and insurance
Where to get supplies and equipment
Where to start to work
When and where to have lunch
Where to smoke and not smoke
Where to make personal phone calls
When to finish shift
How to figure overtime
When and where to pick up pay check
How and where to cash it
Who to call (with phone number) if they are going to be late or absent

Mental Orientation.   In the mental orientation the management will:

Welcome the new employee to the job
Show them where their job fits into the club organization
Convince them they can handle the job

Tell them they will get on-the-job help and will be expected
to ask questions

Convince them they will get along with their coworkers

Sell them on working for this club by discussing fringe benefits, club prospects, and future security

What will their salary be, hourly and how much each week

How many (if any) paid holidays will they receive

If a physical examination is required explain it very carefully and in great detail

UNIONS

American unions have not made a great deal of progress in
unionizing the clubs. This is due to many things:

- good working conditions
- higher pay than the industry average
- unions are very solvent (not hungry for members)
- small numbers of employees located in the individual clubs
- lack of chain operations
- more stable work force

However as the unemployment rate increases, and it will for
the forseeable years, more effort will be expended by all unions
to attract new members. It is therefore mandatory that managers know the following.

Any union has the right to talk to club employees. Therefore nothing is gained by putting stumbling blocks in the
union's way—it only gives the union selling points. Volunteer
to gather all employees in a specific place at noon or after work
so that a union representative may address them. Management
has the right to request a copy of the union's constitution and
bylaws, a roster of its officers, and a statement of its objectives.
When a union files a petition for exclusive representation hire
a labor-management expert. This professional person can save
countless dollars and headaches for management.

EMPLOYEE MOTIVATION

One subject on which everyone has an opinion is "What does
it take to motivate an employee?" The reason is that in dealing

with people, management is faced with the most complicated structure conceivable. Physiologists, psychiatrists, and many learned persons do agree however that motivation in the club business should be in three parts:

1. Management should have the right motivating factors to hire the right people: attractive salary and fringe benefits, beautiful club, cheerful working atmosphere, safe parking facilities, handsome manager, neat lockers, proximity to home. However, the complexity starts when management finds that none of these constitutes the reason an employee started to work. Examples from recent employment interviews revealed these reasons:
   a. Management provided mini skirts and revealing bodice uniforms. This also acted as a reason why the turnover rate in one club was high.
   b. The manager dated his employees and had no objection to the members dating them, both male and female; also reason for turnover.
   c. The employees thought that all members were extremely wealthy and that tips were fabulous.
   d. A man's girlfriend worked at a club and he wanted work so that he could keep "an eye on her."
   e. The club had no bar controls.
   f. The chef controlled the kitchen and if you were one of "his boys" you needed no grocery store.
2. Having the right motivating factors will keep the right people: good training, pleasant surroundings, cheerful coworkers, understanding supervisors, salary sufficiency. However, once again, management is shocked and hurt when good employees resign for job-related reasons such as members were too friendly, members were not friendly enough, work is too difficult, work is not challenging enough. Also there are non-job-related reasons for resignation such as an employee deciding to visit relatives in a distant city, employee's getting married, pregnancy, etc.
3. Having the right motivating factors to encourage employees to improve their job skills is another asset: higher pay grade (thus higher pay), greater responsibility, executive ranks and perquisites. An employee who does not want to be a supervisor and have the additional responsibilities of the job provides the difficult situation in this category.

Management will always try to initiate things in each of the three categories to assist in hiring, keeping, and promoting good employees. It must be kept in mind, however, that one person's cake is another person's ache.

The U.S. Army in their personnel manual has printed a section called Seventeen Ways For a Manager to Motivate His Employees" (U.S. Government Printing Office, Washington, D.C., probably published before ERA became so important!), that is still very useful. Here are some excerpts:

1. Communicate standards and be consistent. This minimizes misdirected efforts and motivates through known goals.
2. Be aware of your own biases and prejudices. Emotional reactions often color what should be objective judgment.
3. Let people know where they stand. Do this consistently through performance evaluations and other methods. To withhold this critical information does the ultimate disservice to your organization (through demotivating the employee) and to the employee, who needs and has a right to know.
4. Give praise when it is appropriate. Properly handled, this is one of the most powerful motivators—especially in difficult performance areas or areas of anxiety.
5. Keep your employees informed of changes that may affect them. This does not mean telling them all activity secrets, but you evidence your own concern for them by informing them of matters in which they are likely to have a direct interest.
6. Care about your employees. Not only be attuned to the individual needs of those under you, but communicate this awareness.
7. Perceive people as ends not means. Avoid the charge of using people for your own selfish goals.
8. Go out of your way to help subordinates. A little extra effort, some personal inconvenience, goes a long way with subordinates in confirming the feeling that what they are doing is important to you— and that they are too. Be sure the help you are giving is what is needed. Remember that in correcting an error, improving a deficiency, or strengthening a weakness, you must first know the individual.
9. Take responsibility for your employees. A part of caring is the willingness to assume some responsibility for what happens to your employees. Be involved in their personal failures as well as their successes. A part of you fails or succeeds with them.
10. Build independence. A supervisor who cares seeks to loosen and gradually drop the reins of supervision. Encourage independent thinking, initiative, resourcefulness.

11. Exhibit personal diligence. The most highly motivated leaders have the most highly motivated followers. "Example" is one of the best motivators.

12. Be tactful with your employees. Consideration, courtesy, sense of balance, appreciation, and sensitivity to the view of others—all are important in dealing with employees.

13. Be willing to learn from others. Give new ideas a friendly reception, even when you know they will not work. This will encourage more creative thinking, and future ideas that may work.

14. Demonstrate confidence. Review any doubts you may have about your department, your staff, your projects, or your organization alone and in private. Demonstration of the Special Services director's confidence builds confidence in his employees. Show by your behavior and speech that you are confident the work can be done; confident of your own responsibility; confident of their ability to handle the job.

15. Allow freedom of expression. Assuming your subordinates are reasonably competent, relax your vigil and allow them freedom to do things their way occasionally. Be more concerned with ultimate results than with methods of accomplishing them. This makes assignments much more interesting and challenging for subordinates.

16. Delegate, delegate, delegate. Assuming your people are competent and ambitious, delegate to them as much of your burden as you can. Recognize that pressure motivates and that most of us are not challenged to perform close to our capacity. Then as much as possible, let them ride with their own decisions, learn from their own mistakes, and revel in their own successes.

17. Encourage ingenuity. The lowest paid clerk may be ingenious. Challenge creativity by urging subordinates to beat your system of doing things. If your filing system is not satisfactory, do not change it yourself, have your clerks and office manager tackle the job. The challenge to improve on the boss's system may bring surprising results.

DELEGATION OF AUTHORITY

The manager is responsible for the day-to-day operation of the club departments, and to do this he must delegate all the authority necessary to his supervisors. The manager plans the acts of every club employee, the supervisor sees that the employee performs in accordance with the plan. Delegation is a difficult management task for a number of reasons but possibly the primary one, from the manager's view, is that it erodes his position. If he or she trains a subordinate to run a particular department well, the board may decide they don't need him. Nothing could be further from the truth; but clubs are plagued with management insecurity and the basic purpose of this text is to provide guidelines to overcome this. Other reasons for the manager's reluctance to delegate are:

1. They are afraid that some of their weaknesses will show. The one thing that cannot be delegated is a guilty conscience. If it exposes poor methods; remember that they were spotlighted by the manaer, not the auditors.
2. They fear competition. If management only understood, they would welcome any supervisor who could take over any of the manager's duties. There are a hundred hours of work for every minute the manager has. If managers will review their responsibilities from Chapter 2 there are so many ways they could increase their value to the club.

The competence of every employee, both supervisors and workers, is a direct compliment to the manager. It must be thought of in this fashion; it must be publicized and it must be visibly appreciated. The manager can praise employees to the members and subtly take credit for their training. The delegation of authority will do many things for the manager. Some of these are:

- The manager owes it to him or herself to delegate responsibilities. It is a form of insurance that the club will run more smoothly and efficiently.
- The manager will have more time to plan.
- The manager will have more peace of mind.
- Delegation builds the manager's image as a ladder.
- The manager owes it to the subordinates to delegate. They must have a chance to exercise authority and manage directly.
- The manager can never hope for promotion to the general manager position or in the commercial club business district, or to a regional manager position unless some subordinate has had some experience in management.

These are the advantages if the manager delegates. On the other side of the coin—what happens when a manager refuses to delegate?

- It puts the supervisors in a worker position if he/she must ask the manager before making any decisions. They cannot gain the respect of their employees unless they can effectively supervise them. Effective supervision is decision making.
- It undermines the supervisors morale.
- It keeps the manager from getting ahead.
- It creates jealousy and mistrust in the entire staff.
- The manager's refusal to delegate frequently means to subordinates that management doesn't trust them. This lack of confidence can be contagious. Time after time it has been observed that minor emergencies will arise and the lack of confidence in subordinate supervisors to make decisions have turned those minor emergencies into major catastrophes. The supervisors will read in management's lack of delegation a lack of caring, a selfishness in the manager, and that perhaps they are personally disliked.

The smart manager will delegate and these are the steps that can be used:

1. Select the jobs that can be delegated and get them organized for turnover. For example, if the manager first interviews all employees prior to their seeing the department head, discontinue the practice, but make sure that everything accomplished in the preliminary interview is explained to the supervisor.
2. Pick the proper person for each job. Some might go to the assistants or night managers, others might go to department heads or supervisors. In one club, the manager liked to clean up his own office. This task was, however, delegated to the janitor with specific instructions on how it was to be done. This janitor appreciated the trust imposed on him.
3. Prepare and motivate the delegates for the assignment. The manager works for him or herself in developing status, prestige, and initiative among his subordinates. Knowledgeable management always delegates work as a compliment and reward for superior performance.

4. Turn over the task and make sure the scope and details are thoroughly understood.

5. Encourage independence. Insist that the employee not report back with progress or results—only with problems.

6. Maintain supervisory control. Never delegate the final responsibility along with the work. The manager is always responsible for everything that happens in the club.

REVIEW QUESTIONS

1. Discuss each of the manager's personnel objectives and ways to accomplish them.

2. Discuss the Reimbursement and Responsibility Chart concept of personnel evaluation:

   a. its composition

   b. its value

   c. its pitfalls

3. Discuss the grade structure in a club and equate various jobs with a progressive grading pattern.

4. Discuss the four types of fringe benefits detailed in the text.

   a. management controlled for all employees

   b. management controlled for selected employees

   c. uncontrollable benefits

   d. imposed by law

5. Discuss and explain the manager's preparation for conducting interviews for club employment.

6. Discuss the details of employee "courtesy training."

7. Discuss and detail the types of principles of motivation.

8. Discuss the need and details of implementation to delegate to subordinate supervisors the authority to hire and fire their staff.

5

Operating

Club

Departments

OVERVIEW

Providing the manager with the technical language of the club business will assist in management communications with the directors, officers, members, and employees of the club.

Some of the recommended operational methods are treated with elaborate detail, others to a lesser degree. The visible aspects of each management component are clearly detailed so that management can make an objective observation and evaluation of them.

The chapter is not intended to teach the manager how to cook, but rather how to evaluate the food department by pinpointing the good and bad things it does.

DEFINITION

In this chapter the manager should find all the information on the day-to-day operation of the club that he or she needs in order to supervise it intelligently. There will be no attempt to train the manager in every facet of every specific job, but rather to provide enough factual information so that each job in the club can be evaluated. For example, this text will not explain how to use a broiler but how immediately to spot whether or not the *employee* knows how. Certain jobs will take more explanation than others. For example, in labor planning some details must be discussed but in the main all subjects are treated in the broadest possible terms.

LABOR PLANNING

The manager, with the supervisors, plans the total operations staff. The staff is divided into full-time and part-time people. It is absolutely essential to keep the full-time staff to those persons who are necessary. They should be a well-trained nucleus of dedicated people who can expand their individual sections on a moment's notice. Labor planning should be accomplished in advance of need and a minimum of one week at a time. This planning is set up in an overall club schedule with details for each department. This could be as follows:

The schedule may be prepared for the waiters and waitresses by the maitre d' and approved by the food and beverage manager. One copy of the schedule is posted where the employees will see it and a copy is sent to payroll. This schedule cannot be changed without the food and beverage manager's approval. This will accomplish some very important things:

1. It is an easy check against the time clock. An employee can clock in at any time but only receives payment in accordance with the schedule.

2. It gives the employee advance notice of his or her working hours for the next week, thereby pinpointing the hours that an employee will have for personal business.

3. It informs the manager of exactly when an employee goes on overtime so that part-time workers can be used.

4. It assists management in scheduling for need not space. Some clubs, because the space is there, schedule for it. For example a West Coast Club has three bars; bartenders are used every day at all three bars, whether they are needed or not. Even after a member complained about the labor waste, the manager did not correct the situation.

Exhibit 5-1. Food and Beverage Department

Employees Name	Date Sunday	Monday	Tuesday	Wednesday	Thursday	Friday	Saturday
Smith	11-2 5-10						

_____   _____
Date   Prepared by

_____   _____
Date   Approved by

The schedule is prepared for the waiters and waitresses by the maitre d' and approved by the Food and Beverage Manager. One copy of the schedule is posted where the employees will see it and one copy is sent to payroll. This schedule cannot be changed without the Food and Beverage Manager's approval.

In preparing the schedule use every bit of information available:

- last year's sales
- last month's sales
- last week's sales
- special events at the club
- special events in the vicinity
- weather, temperature and ground conditions
- member's social and recreation habits

EQUIPMENT USAGE (OUTLINE)

The manager does not need to know how to operate each piece of equipment in the club. But he must know what it will and will not do. He/she must also be aware of the capacity of the equipment and utility of the finished product. For example, it is sometimes very wasteful, and not pleasing to the members, to brew coffee in a five-gallon urn, unless the product, in this case coffee, is used within one hour. The coffee made by the individual-carafe methods of Silex, Cory, etc. are used to produce smaller batches.

The following, a listing of production areas and equipment associated with a basic food and beverage department, is set up as a reference outline:

Food and Beverage Department

Kitchen

Refrigerators and Freezers—These hold the most costly items the club purchases, namely food products. They should be purchased with thermometers built into the outside walls so that the interior temperature can be checked frequently. Expect 32°F(0°C) to 38°F (3°C) in refrigerators, 0°F (−18°C) to 20°F (−6°C) in freezers. Unless the club is unable to get frequent deliveries a walk-in freezer should not be purchased. If the club has a freezer, convert it to a walk-in refrigerator. In many clubs the walk-in freezer is a very expensive garbage box.

The manager should also consider standby generators with automatic switch-over devices that start the generators if power fails or fluctuates. Power failures are very visible, current fluctuations are not. The manager should require the power company to set a recording voltameter on the club line at least twice a year.

All merchandise must be stored on racks and all refrigerators should be emptied and cleaned on a regular basis.

Ice Makers—Ice is the heart of the bar operation and an important part of the food section. Managers must understand the ice needs of the club and these needs must be satisfied by in-house manufacture. Many machines have a capacity far greater than their storage bins, and in some clubs a home chest-type freezer has been a very profitable investment. It is also sanitarily effective to empty the bin for cleaning purposes.

Broilers—The club broiler will use any one of three types of fuel, all burning at different temperatures. These are charcoal, gas, and electricity. All should have one mechanical adjustment to change the height of the broiling rack from the heat source. The user can also use the heat source to create hot and warm spots on the rack with other adjustments. Since high temperatures tends to seal meats so that they retain their natural juices, a good broiler operator:

1. starts meats with the broil rack close to the heat source
2. gradually raises the rack so the meat comes to the desired degree of doneness without burning
3. turns the meat with a spatula or tongs so the crust of the meat is not pierced

Char-broilers use the heat source to burn meat drippings into a smoke which rises and adds distinctive flavors to the broiled item.

Griddles—These can be solid so that eggs can be scrambled and items fried, or slotted for cooking with pots and pans. The manager must see that the griddle is frequently cleaned during the day. A good griddle operator checks the thermostat between every cooking use to make sure the temperature is correct. Also the operator must check the surface temperature, the management furnishing the cook with good thermometers for this purpose.

Ovens—The manager must consider the ovens in the club as versatile pieces of equipment. Every cooked item that the restaurant serves can be prepared for human consumption in an oven. Ovens with individually controlled top and bottom elements can do roasting, baking, broiling, and boiling. Although this last use would be strictly for emergencies, it is safe to say the oven will perform every cooking function except frying. The oven should be equipped with a fan to even out the heat, cut shrinkage, and speed up the cooking process. Commercially these are called *convectaire* ovens.

Microwave ovens are used to speed service and cut waste.

Terms that the manager must know in using ovens are:

Rotary revolving rack type used by bakeries, in commercial food preparation, and large restaurants.

Deck ovens that can be stacked so that a "two deck," "three deck," "four deck oven" would mean ovens stacked 2, 3, and 4 high.

Microwave an oven that uses radiant energy, known as microwaves. This heat penetrates non-metallic surfaces and the energy is absorbed by the products, which are heated by internal friction. The time needed to prepare most items is cut by 80 percent. One of the early drawbacks to this oven was that heating from within would not carmelize the meat surface to give them the appearance of roasts. This has been corrected in later models by adding a conventional heating element.

Slow Roasting/Baking and Holding a kind of oven, invented in the '70s, that cuts meat shrinkage and labor. Roasts can be prepared and placed in the oven when the dining room closes at night and be roasted and held at the proper temperature and be ready for carving the next day. The trade name for this oven is "Alta Sham."

Mixer—For the typical club kitchen needing small table-top mixers (no larger than four- to six-quart capacity), these are labor savers and do a multitude of mixing jobs. The sizes are even large enough for the club to make its own quick breads, rolls, and pastries.

Steam-Pressure Cooker—This is primarily used for vegetable cookery, but has other uses. These can be stove top or self-contained. The self-contained ones are recommended for the clubs. The manager must know he is dealing with super-heated steam and train employees in detail on the removal of the food stuffs from the machine.

Soft Ice Cream Machines—More and more these machines are replacing regular ice cream in the clubs. The reasons for this are:

- speed of service
- multiple usages
- sundaes are simpler to make
- a la mode for pies and cakes
- toppings for custards, jellos, etc.
- profit (cost is less than ice cream but product is very acceptable to the member)

Kettle—Originally used for mass food production, kettles were manufactured in huge sizes of 20, 40, 60, and 80 gallons (75.6, 151.2, 226.8 and 302.4 liters) and larger. The modern club uses much smaller kettles. A kettle can use steam or electricity as a heat source. Most are on a gimbel-type bracket that allows them to be tilted for each product removal. These that swivel are called trunion kettles and come in one gallon (3.78 liters) and up. Kettles are used to cook many items such as soups, vegetables, desserts, etc. and are very useful in the kitchen. They must be cleaned after every use.

Fryer—The deep-fat fryer is probably, with the oven, the oldest piece of cooking equipment known to man. It is a very difficult machine to use and requires a great deal of training to operate properly. The temperature and cleanliness of the fat are crucial to a good finished product. If the temperature is too low the product absorbs the grease; if too high, the product burns. If the grease is dirty, it affects the flavor of the product. The fat must be strained at least daily, and the fryer and baskets cleaned.

There are many "automatic" fryers offered by manufacturers that have definite advantages over the manual ones. However they still must be checked constantly as the thermostats are not nearly as well engineered as the equipment.

Food Chopper—This is sometimes called a "Buffalo" and is used for chopping, dicing, and shredding. The manager must know that the principle of this machine is rapidly whirling steel blades. It must never be operated without the guards being attached. It requires cleaning after each use.

Grinder—This is a very handy and economical machine to have in the club kitchen. If the club is using quality beef there will be trimmings that can be turned into hamburger. Boneless beef, ground on the premises, assures absolute quality control of hamburger, croquettes, etc. The knives must be sharp, a pusher must be chained to the machine, and it must be disassembled and cleaned after each use.

Meat Slicer—This machine is used for slicing food products. The uniformity of the slices assists in controlling portions, thus controlling costs. The manager should encourage the use of the machine for larger-bulk meat items such as rib roasts, turkeys breasts, etc. It must be cleaned after each use.

Dishwashing Machine—A dish machine will sanitize and clean dishes, glassware, and silverware if operated properly. The items should sparkle—management should insist on this. It is a complex machine but operates on a very simple principle. Water at the proper temperature and mixed with a cleaning agent is sprayed under pressure over the items. Then they are hit again by water mixed with a water-sheathing agent. These are known as the washing and rinsing cycles. Sparkling results are accomplished by the following:

- The temperature of the wash water must be no colder than 130°F (54°C) nor hotter than 140°F (60°C). If the water temperature is lower than 130°F (54°C) some foods cannot be sprayed off; if it is hotter than 140°F (60°C) some foods will be cooked on.
- The water is sprayed from revolving pipes with small holes in them. The pipes must be cleaned daily, the bottom pipes maybe more

often, so that they are free from food debris that might cover the holes.

- A good detergent or soap powder must be fed into the water in preset quantities. Too little or too much will not work efficiently. The pump that provides this feeding must be checked at least weekly. Most companies that sell cleaning products provide this as a free service. The knowledgeable manager does not purchase from a company that does not provide this.

- The temperature of the rinse water must be at least 180°F (82°C). This sanitizes the items, destroys almost all harmful bacteria. The rinse nozzles must also be cleaned daily. The manager must not confuse sanitizing with sterilizing, which takes water temperature of at least 212°F (100°C) and is not necessary.

- The rinse injector and the sheathing solution must be in working order for the items to sparkle and not show "water spots." The solution is also known as a drying agent. The secret of the sparkle is fast drying.

- Using the racks and cups properly is essential. The racks provide a place for each item of china and glassware, with silverware in the cups. If they are overloaded by placing items on top of each other, the machine does not clean properly.

The Air-Exhaust and Exchange Systems—These are the fans, blowers, and other equipment that make the kitchen safe and workable. Also from the members' standpoint they eliminate kitchen odors. There are certain types of kitchen equipment that require venting. The manager is responsible for the fans, etc. working properly. Too little venting produces unwelcome heat and odors. Too much venting results in huge energy waste when too much heat is drawn off the equipment. Every kitchen should be checked by a competent engineer at least annually. The signs of trouble a manager looks for are:

- a drastic difference in temperature between the dining room and kitchen
- clouds of steam above any piece of equipment
- paint peeling above any piece of equipment
- water condensation on floors, walls, or ceiling

Thermostats and Gauges—The poorest parts of any equipment manufactured prior to 1975 are the thermostats and

temperature gauges. The finest working equipment with un-
reliable controls is a menace to product and personnel. At least
weekly the manager must check or have the chef check all
built-in controls with portable thermometers.

Garbage and Trash Disposal Equipment and Systems—The
disposal of garbage and trash is a management problem. The
club disposal system should start with a garbage grinder installed in the dishwashing scraping table. This should be
equipped with magnetic controls so that silverware is not
scraped along with the waste food. All garbage regardless of its
source (bar, office, etc.) should go into the machine. Conditions
may not, however, allow a grinder, and garbage may have to be
stored for later collection. In these cases use plastic bags as
liners for garbage cans instead. If these bags have to be stored
inside the club awaiting collection they should be refrigerated.
Management should make every effort to contract for pickup
that provides a huge container that is convenient to, but outside, the kitchen for the garbage and trash.

Trash consists of all the dry disposable products the club
generates. Boxes, cans, bottles, and paper are bulky, attract
insects and rodents, and exhude odors. A trash impactor which
crushes, packs, and deodorizes trash is a good investment. This
piece of equipment can usually amoritize its cost by reducing
the expense of trash removal.

The additional equipment that the club kitchen needs in
addition to that listed in Chapter 3 is provided as a management check-off list.

Condiment rack	Shelving
Quartz plate warmers	Draining racks
Guest check holder	Tool rack
Kitchen hand tools	Pots and pans
Knives	Plate covers
Skimmers	Drinking fountain
Ladles	Utensil rack
Spoons	Food checker's stand with cash
Forks	resgister
Strainers	Adequate lighting

Dining Room

In addition to the chairs, tables, and the table service of china, glassware, silverware, and linen, the dining room needs:

Waiters Stations—These are sideboards or other pieces of furniture where a coffee hot plate can be set up, spare china, glassware, silverware, and linen can be held for ready use. In addition it saves labor if it also has running water, ice, and refrigerated space for desserts.

Other materials should include:

- a dessert cart
- folding waiter's stands
- flower and bud vases
- ash trays
- flowers
- maitre d's stand with light
- dimmer switches for all lights

Bar and Cocktail Lounge

The manager's responsibility in this area is to serve the best drink economically possible, provide good service, and make a profit. To serve the "best drink," a standard recipe must be established and bartenders given the necessary equipment to prepare it. The most costly and most important ingredient in the majority of mixed drinks served is the alcoholic beverage it contains. Therefore if the recipe calls for an ounce and a half (4.44ml) of scotch for a scotch and soda the bartender must have a device for measuring this amount quickly and exactly, and pouring it from the bottle to the glass.

The equipment available for the manager's selection in measuring devices runs from a small measuring glass (called a jigger) to very sophisticated electronic devices.

Other than the "jigger" the mechanical devices are of two types. One is gravity flow where the measuring device is attached to the bottle lip and acts as a flow-meter for the beverage. The other is an electronic pump that sucks the beverage from the bottle. The three types each have advantages and disadvantages that the manager must know.

Jigger—It is slow, not completely accurate due to the bartender's having to hurry but it does add some glamour to the bar.

Gravity Flow—There are two types, one where the bartender actually handles the bottle; the other has the bottles locked in a rack. Some pourers are faster than the jiggers, some slower. All have one advantage and that is that every drink poured is recorded. The type attached to the bottle makes some brands (because of bottle shape) top heavy and awkward to handle.

Electronic Systems—There are many types of these available and the bottles can either be located at the bar or in a storeroom. The bottles can be hooked in tandem so that replacement is no problem. They are very fast in dumping the right measurement into the glass and make for easy accountability. They are a major investment and the cost must be equated with the volume of sales and the "risk factors." A portable bar can be equipped with this type of device and adds to an intimate atmosphere for a party as the guests can serve themselves. New machines have cash registers and inventory attachments so that a bartender can record the sale and have the product poured in one operation. The last advantage of a pump is that it overcomes the natural capillary attraction of the bottle and completely empties it. This cannot be done in any other fashion.

Draft-Beer Machines—There are two kinds of draft beer systems and machines.

Economy box—a refrigerator and tap where the barrel of beer is cooled and dispensed with the aid of a tank of carbon-dioxide gas. It is a good, very economical system but it has limitations. It should be noted that the refrigerator can only hold one or two barrels of beer and when these are emptied service is interrupted. The box must be serviced from behind the bar. Thus the keg must be transported behind the bar, put in the box, and connected. In many clubs this necessitates bringing the beer through the cocktail lounge.

Remote draw—a better system to hold the beer in a refrigerated box, readily accessible to the delivery area that delivers the beer to the bar through refrigerated lines. The beer and the tap can be 100 feet apart without affecting the quality of the product. The barrels can be hooked in series and any production load can be established.

*Beer Coolers—*If bottle or canned beer is to be sold in the bar, coolers will be needed. There are many types available but all require the same supervision. The boxes must be kept clean and the beer stock must be continually rotated. Each time the cooler is stocked all the beer should be removed, the box cleaned, the fresh beer put in first, and then the beer that was taken from the box put back in on top.

Other equipment needed in the bar and cocktail lounge would be

- a blender; this would be used for some exotic mixed drink and all frozen drinks
- a coffee hot plate for a carafe of coffee
- fruit pans
- cash register
- double sinks
- cold water-glass washer
- speed rail
- glassware including shot glasses
- ash trays
- paper goods, napkins, coasters, straws, toothpicks
- paring knives and spear-type forks
- hot and cold running water
- a bar and back bar
- bar stools
- tables and chairs

Recreation Department

Golf Division

The most expensive pieces of equipment in this division are the golf carts, the trucks, and the mowing machines. A record must be maintained on the original cost of each machine, as well as its maintenance. This becomes a little complicated with electrical equipment as the manufacturers' figures on both electrical usage and recharge rarely approach the actual costs. If at all possible get the recharge line for this equipment set up through a meter.

There could also be shoe, club, bag and ball cleaning and repair equipment.

Tennis Division

This division has ball-throwers and sometimes line-marking machines. There also may be restringing, racket repairing, and tennis-ball pressure machines. Inventories should be maintained on all club-owned gear.

Swimming Division

This division would be responsible for the pool-side furniture, life-saving equipment, and the pool-pumping system. Maintain a detailed inventory and if this division is seasonal, have indoor storage set up for all furniture and portable gear.

Retail Sales Department

Hotel/Motel Division

In addition to the room furnishings, cleaning equipment such as maids' carts, vacuum cleaners, floor polishing and buffing machines must be maintained. Detailed inventories must be maintained for all these items.

Pro and Gift Shop Division

In addition to the display cases and racks, the shops might carry a complete line of rental equipment. All resale merchandise should be controlled by the retail-accountability method.

Support Department

This department should have office equipment including desks, chairs, typewriters, calculators, adding machines, etc. A record should be maintained for each machine showing date of purchase, purchase price, and listing any repairs with their costs.

Maintenance Department

This department should have hand and other types of tools. In many clubs carpenter and other type shops are set up for building and equipment maintenance. All equipment should be recorded and a "tool crib" system set up for issuing tools to the workmen.

PLANNING THE SERVICE OFFERED

The management plans the services that will be offered to the members according to members' needs and desires. However, the problem arises when these services are beyond the financial capacity of the club. Therefore management must determine what will be offered by presenting an operating budget to the board of directors for approval.

The preparation of the operating budget is completely separate from the financial statement. In the budget, every charge that is part of the overhead is an operating expense for each income-producing department.

The club manager, unlike his counterpart in the rest of the hospitality industry, has a possible subsidy for each department. These subsidies come from the dues the members pay. The budget estimates that a particular department will generate 75 percent of its cost unless service was curtailed or prices raised. The members may be satisfied with this and subsidize the other 25 percent by allocating this amount from dues.

It is a management responsibility to have records so that income and costs can be determined. In divisions that are marginal, hourly cash register readings could be recorded to determine the busiest hours. This can easily be done by marking the cash register tape.

The ideal that management strives for is to stay solvent and serve food and beverages from daybreak to at least midnight, seven days a week, and to have all facilities open from sunrise to sunset, with all lighted facilities available to the members until at least midnight. However, the members determine this by their patronage and financial strength.

The manager, in addition to cost of goods sold, labor, and expenses, must also know the number of members who use the facility. This would then allow the allocation of overhead percentages to each of the revenue-producing departments. For example, based on the premise that the club's sole purpose is to provide relaxation and recreation for its members, a basic cost of these services represents the expenses for the support and maintenance departments, management, and all other overhead expenses. The manager accummulates the data from golf-starting time, reservations, score cards, tennis court reservations, swimming pool attendants' records, guest checks, bartenders count, room registration cards, estimates from usage, etc. The manager then applies the percentage of usage to the total memership:

> 70% of the membership use the golf course
> 50% use the tennis courts
> 25% use the swimming pool
> 60% use the food and beverage department
> <u>80%</u> use the retail sales
>
> 285% Total

The percent of usage for budget purposes is determined by dividing the total of these percentages into the percent of use. The percentages management would work with are:

> 24% overhead charged to golf
> 17% to tennis
> 9% to swimming
> 21% to food and beverage
> 29% to retail sales

This system determines the budgeted planning cost for each department and division. With the estimate of income based on sales forecasting, the entire financial picture is complete. In commercial-type clubs, the expected return on dollar invested would be an expense added to overhead.

Management of an ongoing club, by using this approach, could present a complete analysis to the board. In a new club alternatives could be offered. This is presented as follows:

Dining room open seven days a week—

Breakfast	6:30 A.M. to	9:00 A.M.	Mon–Sat
Luncheon	11:00 A.M. to	2:00 P.M.	Mon–Sat
Dinner	5:00 P.M. to	11:00 P.M.	Sun –Sat
Estimated monthly income		$40,000	
Estimated monthly expense		55,000	
Expenses over income		$15,000	

Dining room open six days a week with the same operating hours but closed on Monday—

Estimated monthly income	$37,000
Estimated monthly expense	49,000
Expenses over income	$12,000

With the figures available, management could present as many alternatives as the board desired.

INVENTORY PLANNING

It is necessary to plan the inventory in every department and division or there will be too much or too little of many items. The inventory must be managed by a professional purchasing agent under the direct supervision of the comptroller. This is one reason for retail accountability in the bar, snack bar, and shops as this system pinpoints usage. With food guest checks absolutely accurate data is given on product used. Inventory must be planned with high and low stock levels. These figures are then the planning factors for the placing of the purchase order. For example, a very popular golf shirt may be cream colored, in men's size fifteen-and-a-half, with short sleeves. The purchasing agent, knowing delivery time, will determine that fifteen is the "high" for this product, three the "low." When the inventory level reaches three the clerk code-marks the sales slip from the identification data on the tag and shelf. The cost-control clerk informs the purchasing agent and a dozen shirts are ordered.

PURCHASING

A wise man once said, "the easiest dollars you will ever earn are those you save by good purchasing." Purchasing is not only important from a profit standpoint but the quality of the raw product will control, in most instances, the finished product that is served to the member.

Purchasing is a complex business. Quite often the cheapest merchandise is not the most profitable! For example, in buying produce, when a twenty-head case of lettuce, US Fancy, is $4.00, it may be much more profitable than a case graded lower than Fancy at $3.50 in terms of the waste due to the poorer quality. Therefore, purchasing must always be judged by its over-all effectiveness and never by the price paid for any one article.

The technique of good buying is divided into the following six factors:

1. the purchaser
2. purchasing ethics
3. purchasing methods
4. purchasing sources
5. what to purchase
6. using purchase orders

The person responsible for expending funds for the operation occupies an increasingly important position as labor and other costs rise. This key individual must know the ingredients used to prepare the items on the menu (or have this information supplied to him), know something about food preparation, and be fully aware of the other five purchasing factors. Thus, in order to do an efficient job, the purchaser must be a person with experience in the food business.

The second consideration a good purchaser must keep in mind is time. Does the individual selected have time enough to do an intelligent job? He must accumulate prices, study local marketing practices, be alert for new products, be familiar with market trends, work closely with the chef, interview salesmen, and keep a constant watch on regular sales and special events.

Next, does he have the personality to get agreements easily from other persons? This is important because, in his day-to-day relationship with the business, he is frequently the bridge between the vendor and his own production department. For example, a certain food item is in season and in plentiful supply. The purchaser must convince the chef to serve it if he is to utilize this potential fully. He must have the poise to meet the vendor salesman on a friendly basis yet maintain a strict businesslike relationship.

The final qualification is that the buyer must be loyal and honest. His integrity will be put to the test on occasion as certain unscrupulous salesmen attempt to "buy his business" or influence his judgement with personal favors. Fortunately this is not widespread in the food business and is easily detected by alert management, because of the high competitiveness of the product.

The successful purchaser must understand and abide by recognized ethical practices. It is quite proper to shop the market and discuss prices or trends with a vendor as long as he does not "chisel." Chiseling is the trade term for beating the vendors down by disclosing the price offered by his competitors, or by telling the vendor his price is too high. A far faster, more subtle and effective method is to train the vendors to quote one price, the lowest they can offer. This is accomplished by the activities-purchasing methods.

The purchaser's code of ethics should be guided by the following:

1. He will not disclose the price quoted him by any other vendor to another vendor.

2. He will not ask the vendor to reduce the price of any product to meet competition or menu needs. He, of course, can establish his needs and ask the vendor for products to fulfill them.

3. He will give every purveyor the opportunity to quote prices to him.

4. He will be loyal to his employer.

5. He will exhibit the nicest degree of honesty to his employer and to all vendors.

6. He will accept no personal favors or gifts from any vendor.

There are many methods that may be used to buy items for the restaurant but the usual ones used by clubs are:

Approved Vendors—A manager who cannot do all of the purchasing himself delegates the authority and responsibility to subordinates. He does this in writing and directs the Purchasing agent, the chef, bartender, and others that they may only purchase items from the vendor's listed. This list is compiled by visiting the various clubs in the area and finding out which vendors are supplying them. Also through the local CMAA chapter, managers could get recommendations of those vendors known to supply quality products at a reasonable price, and to observe ethical practices. From these and other sources an approved list is established and the purchaser is restricted to vendors on it. New suppliers get on the list by proving their dependability at other clubs first.

Open Purchasing—This is the method of purchasing on the market from the vendor who can supply the highest quality items for the lowest price. The usual procedure is to determine the items needed and list them on the market-quotation form. A separate form is used for each class of items. Then the purchasing agent contacts the approved dealers and fills in the prices quoted by each one. A study is then made to determine the best price and quality and purchase orders are prepared. If the vendor is allowed to quote only one price he soon learns to quote the club the lowest one.

Sealed Bids—This is the method of purchasing in which the needs of the club are determined in advance. A list with an invitation to bid is forwarded to the proper vendors. The invitation contains, in addition to the items and their quantities, the date the bids will be opened, all delivery information, whether individual items or the total are being bid upon, and the time limit of the contract.

This method is highly recommended for competitive items such as dairy and bakery products.

Commercial vendors are normally divided into three categories—packers or manufacturers, prefabricators, and jobbers (though there is sometimes an overlap in that a packer may also be a fabricator). The packers or manufacturers are those companies who purchase the live animal or raw product and reduce

Exhibit 5-2. Market Quotation Form

Date

Items Needed	Quantity	Details	Produce Co #1	Produce Co #2	Produce Co #3
Tomatoes	5 lugs	#1 Fancy			
Lettuce	6 cases	Fancy			
Endive	10 baskets				
Radishes	25 bunches				
Cucumbers	1 crate				

it to its accepted commercial form. The prefabricators (mainly in the meat business) buy the commercial cuts of meat—rounds, loins, chucks, and ribs, and reduce these to individual portion servings. The jobbers purchase and accumulate various items of merchandise, sometimes in carload lots, and sell the items to the club in the quantity needed. In some areas there is a fourth category of vendor—the local farmer.

The purchaser will be buying equipment, furnishings, food, alcoholic beverages, and supplies.

In the purchase of equipment or furnishings a master plan is always helpful. This allows increment purchasing as funds become available that will accomplish an overall renovation. Before any new items are purchased it must be determined whether an old piece can be rehabilitated.

The purchaser should make a practice of attending the National Restaurant Show in Chicago, or regional show, or the National Hotel Show in New York City to be sure he knows the newest types of products and equipment.

When buying food, the bulletins from the US Department of Agriculture are helpful. These "Plentiful Foods Monthly Lists" publicize the items of food that are in abundance. Because of the law of supply and demand, this fact usually indicates that they will be reduced in price. Thus the items to be bought and featured on your menu are suggested each month. These bulletins are available by requesting them from the nearest regional office of the Department of Agriculture. Offices are located in New York City, Chicago, San Francisco, Atlanta, and Dallas.

Meats should be purchased in accordance with the "Standarized Meat Cuts" as suggested by the National Association of Hotel and Restaurant Meat Purveyors (Suite 1728, 120 S. Riverside Plaza, Chicago, Ill. 60606). Their book, which has been endorsed by the US Department of Agriculture, is available without charge.

Provisions, seafood, poultry, dairy, and bakery products, vegetables and fruit, either fresh, canned or frozen, should be purchased according to the specifications published by the US Government. This information is available in many professional food-service books.

Food and beverages should always be purchased in the size that the kitchen or bar uses. For example, if the kitchen uses flour in five-pound increments it should be purchased in five-pound bags. It has been noted that buying items in sizes larger than needed greatly increases waste.

Successful management requires that, whenever possible, all purchasing be recorded on purchase-order forms. The forms become an integral part of the internal-control system and also accomplish the following:

1. Establishes a contractual relationship between the club and the vendors as well as a customer/purveyor relationship.
2. Provides a document upon which good receiving procedures may be based.
3. Provides ready reference for pricing daily requisitions and breakouts.
4. Provides a control document for payment of accounts payable.
5. Provides a record of the contingent liabilities and accounts payable of the club.

In addition to the instructions on the form a "dispute clause" should be included so that any disagreements between the club and the vendor could be arbitrated.

The form requires a minimum of four copies, with a copy to the vendor, the bookkeeper, the storekeeper, or receiving section.

The bookkeeper's copy is used as a control on the invoice and accounts payable. The storekeeper certifies that the merchandise has been received on one copy, which is forwarded to the main office, and retains one copy for his records.

In conclusion, if the purchaser studies and practices the six purchasing factors he can contribute immeasurably to the successful operation of the club.

HOLDING

The purpose of planned food holding is:

1. to hold fresh food products in as close a state as possible to their original receipt
2. to keep food frozen until it is time to start preparations.
3. to have the canned and packaged foods required by the menu on hand
4. to have all products readily available to the kitchen
5. to reduce food costs to a minimum

The problems involved in the planning and management of holding spaces are sometimes aggravated by factors beyond the control of the staff. These can be poor equipment, lack of proper types of storage, poor location, and many others. In this text holding food is that period of time between the receipt of the product and its issuance to the kitchen. The holding of prepared food and leftovers will be covered in "Food Preparation."

The following factors must be considered if management is to improve the storing of food:

- location of holding areas
- equipment in the areas
- sanitation and safety in the areas
- stock stowage in the areas

- security of areas
- training the storekeeper

The holding areas for food can be divided into the following:

Freeze Reach-In Box—This space should be the coldest one available where temperatures can be kept at 0°F (−18°C) or colder. This space will be used to store all frozen foods. After freezing, food need not be separated into its various categories as they will not impart flavors to each other.

Chill Walk-In Boxes—These spaces will be used to store meat, fresh fruits and vegetables, seafood, strong cheeses, and to thaw frozen foods. The temperature of these boxes should be from 30°F (−1°C) to 40°F (4°C). The ideal arrangement would be to have one box 30°F (−1°C) to 35°F (2°C) and another 31°F (−1°C) to 40°F (4°C).

Dairy Box—This area will be used to store milk, butter, mild cheese, dry yeast, and eggs. The temperature in this box should range from 31°F (−1°C) to 33°F (1°C).

Ice Cream Box—This area will be used to store ice cream and sherbets at a temperature of at least 0°F (−18°C).

Dry-Provision Holding Room—This room will be used to hold provisions that do not require refrigeration. The temperature should be from 50°F (10°C) to 70°F (21°C).

There are some basic "do's":

1. Examine all foods frequently for signs of spoilage and, with the supervisor's permission, remove foods from the inventory. Check for rust spots or bulges on cans, spoiled meats, and vegetables, etc.
2. Stow similar foods in the same area but be carful not to overstack. Usually "five high" is a good stacking rule. Check to see that all items are stowed in their proper places and at the proper temperature.
3. Wipe up immediately any food or grease that is spilled.
4. Check all holding areas with a flashlight for insects, rodents, and as necessary, take proper corrective action.

Here are some basic "don't's":

1. Do not allow open or uncovered boxes or cans to remain in the room, but issue them to the kitchen so that they can be used.

2. Do not stack or hang meat or vegetable items so close that air cannot circulate around them.
3. Do not open or leave refrigerator door ajar any longer than necessary.
4. Do not allow ice to form on the reefer coils but get either automatic defrosting equipment installed or set up a manual defrosting cycle.
5. Do not put items other than food or food-service gear in the food spaces. Open drums of wax, furniture polish, kerosene, or paint may impart their odors to food.

STOCK STORAGE

Stowing the food in its proper storage area is considered in two parts: first, where to hold food and second, how to hold it. The ideal refrigeration setup would be to have five available temperatures:

Ice Cream box	$0°F$ $(-18°C)$
Freeze box	$0°F$ $(-18°C)$
Meat box	$30°F$ to $35°F$ $(-1°C$ to $2°C)$
Dairy box	$31°F$ to $33°F$ $(-1°C$ to $1°C)$
Vegetable box	$31°F$ to $40°F$ $(-1°C$ to $4°C)$
Dry provision room	$50°F$ to $70°F$ $(10°C$ to $21°C)$

Ice cream will keep from six to nine months at $10°F$ $(-12°C)$ or below, but all flavors except chocolate will eventually lose their fresh taste and texture.

Frozen meat should be wrapped and packed solidly on shelves. When packed in boxes, the boxes should be unopened until ready for use. When a box is opened, it should be resealed after the desired quantity of meat is removed. Remember that frozen food is not sterile but that some bacteria form spores and continue to live in a dormant stage. As the food thaws they regain all of their toxic potentials.

Poultry tends to lose flavor when held in a frozen state and the life-expectancy table should be rigidly adhered to. Each bird must be individually wrapped, sealed, and hard frozen.

Fish and seafood items are divided into fatty fish, and herring, and the less-fatty ones like flounder, sea bass, cod, haddock, smelt, and pike. The fatty fish along with shrimp are very perishable and unless kept at 0°F (−18°C) and below will quickly spoil.

Frozen fruits, juices, and vegetables can be held at temperatures of 10°F (−12°C) and below without danger of loss.

Fresh meat, or meat to be thawed, should be held in a chill box at a temperature of from 30°F (−1°C) to 35°F (2°C). The desirable humidity is from 85 to 90 percent to keep shrinkage at a minimum. Air circulation around all items is very important. Use meat hooks on rails and make sure that items do not touch each other.

Fresh oysters, clams, lobsters, and crabs must be kept alive to the time of preparation but can be held in the chill box.

Strong cheeses such as Limburger, Gorgonzola, American Blue, Roquefort, Parmesan, and Camembert should be well wrapped and held in the chill box.

The dairy box will be used for milk, butter, mild cheese, dry yeast, and eggs. Be sure to mark the date received on all items. Much care should be given to holding, making sure the temperature is correct and supplies are not openly exposed to air currents. Keep butter wrapped as it also picks up odors.

Eggs will be cross stacked with slates in between tiers to assure air circulation. Always stack cases right-side up. Eggs are placed with the pointed end, which is the strongest, down. Eggs should be placed in the coldest part, or rear of the box. Egg shells being porous will absorb other food odors. Date each case recieved with a grease pencil so that the oldest stock is always used first.

Compressed yeast retains its baking strength if kept around 30°F (−1°C). Place this item at the rear of the box also.

The vegetable box should be used to hold all fresh fruits and vegetables that require refrigeration. Produce should be inspected often for signs of spoilage. One bad item will cause all items touching it to spoil. Although they need a certain amount of moisture to prevent excessive drying, fruits and vegetables spoil more quickly when they are wet. The moisture inside the box may be increased by hanging several clean wet burlap bags near the chill-box blower. When items are individually wrapped do not remove these wrappers until the item is served. Fresh vegetables and fruits emit respiration gases which can flavor foods high in liquid content, including cooked foods. They themselves can also be contaminated by absorbing flavors from other foods. All vegetables in cases, when more than one case is purchased at a time (such as lettuce, celery, etc.) should be dated upon receipt.

Fruits and vegetables that should be held under refrigeration are divided into two classes: those that require the bottom range of temperatures in the box, and those that require the top. Checking with a thermometer will tell you the cold spots in the box as the airflow directly affects the temperature.

White potatoes, if earmarked for french fries, should be held at a temperature of 70°F (21°C) for at least two weeks before using. Potatoes held at 50°F (10°C) or below change their potato starch content to sugar, become too sweet with an objectionable sugar flavor, and will brown too quickly.

Canned goods should be stowed in a dry, low-humidity area, around 50°F (10°C). Never use rusted or bulged cans as the contents may be contaminated. The bulge always indicates that the product has spoiled. Sometimes cans that have been stored develop tiny holes without rusting; these must not be used. Cans containing evaporated milk require special care. This product keeps best at 60°F (15°C).

Baking power, cornstarch, crackers, macaroni, spaghetti, and baking soda must be protected from moisture and excessive heat.

Dried beans and barley require a cool spot to avoid sweating. Make sure they are well ventilated.

Water-ground cornmeal requires special attention as it can turn rancid quickly. Flour should be stored by itself, if possible, since it absorbs odors and moisture. Flour begins to deteriorate at temperatures over 75°F (24°C) when molds and bacteria start to grow.

Prunes, raisins, and other dry fruits do not require refrigeration.

Rice has a tendency to dry out in storage and lose weight. This does not affect its taste or food value. But it tends to become musty and will develop a bad taste unless ventilated.

Candy will develop white "bloom" at temperatures over

70°F (21°C). This does not affect its taste or spoil the candy. Its appearance, however, is much less appetizing.

Spices lose their flavor if exposed to air. Pickles in glass jars will become discolored if exposed to the light. Light also affects flavoring extracts, making them lose their flavor.

Mayonnaise, mustard, salad dressing, tomato catsup, and chili sauce will keep best at a moderate temperature not to exceed 60°F (15°C). These items will discolor if exposed to direct sunlight. Mayonnaise that receives rough treatment will lose much of its smooth texture.

SECURITY

Thinking of food as money seems to be the best approach to safeguarding it. In establishing adequate security measures, the storekeeper must be able to answer the following hypothetical questions positively:

1. If the end of the month inventory shows that merchandise is missing, can the items that are missing be determined?
2. Can one person be held accountable for missing items?
3. Does the management know at all times who has the keys to the locked holding spaces?
4. Is there a regular breakout time for each meal?
5. Are all items that are removed from the holding room recorded? If not, is there some other control system in effect?
6. Is access to the holding room limited only to personnel who have business there?
7. Is the food inventory kept as low as possible?

Keeping the inventory dollar value low is important and can be accomplished by buying only for the menu. "Good buys," unless the menu can be changed for the current periods, may have all their advantages trimmed away because they were held too long! Overstocking has these hazards or disadvantages:

- foods may spoil
- funds are tied up

- inventory taking is slower
- a tendency to be careless in issuing may be created
- food may be stolen

TRAINING THE STOREKEEPER

The next factor is the extensive training of the storekeeper. He must be taught to receive and stow. He must be motivated to take a personal and intelligent interest in the job, and a great pride in doing it well. As the employee starts to understand and appreciate the technology of the business, he will find many ways to better protect the club investment.

RECEIVING

The well-managed club must take the time and effort to establish receiving procedures. It is normal, for an otherwise well-managed business, sometimes to completely overlook receiving. This very essential part of any operation is considered to be a part of the vendor's obligation. The vendor delivers and often actually places the purchases in their storage area. Thus, the handling having passed to the vendor's hands, it is easy to believe that the responsibility for the safe delivery of the goods has also been assumed. Nothing could be further from the truth.

The restaurant industry pays many dollars each year for merchandise that is never delivered. Therefore, it is vitally important to consider receiving as one of the major components of the restaurant business.

In studying the techniques of receiving, it is pertinent to consider goods as money, and that money is a very fluid commodity. Money flows into the establishment through the front door (dollars of members) and the back door (dollars of goods). The front-door money is usually very well protected in at least four ways:

1. by having only carefully selected personnel handle it
2. by cash registers and standard cash handling procedures

3. by prenumbered sales slips

4. by other forms of controls

But the back-door money? That's so different! Too often the bread man is actually in the kitchen replacing stale bread with fresh without any close observation. The milkman, another fellow trusted over and above the club's own employees, brings his product in, places it in a refrigerator, and usually gets a receipt for delivery or products the signer has never seen. Next, however, is the real problem person—the meatman. Here's the chap who can make any profit he desires on any selling price if he is unscrupulous. Consider pork loins selling at 90 cents per pound; if the charge is for 100 pounds, but only 99 pounds are received, there is an out of pocket loss of 90 cents. If 98 pounds are received, the loss is $1.80, and on and on. Weight is also used to adjust prices. Salesmen, in order to meet competition, have been known to make up the price difference by short weight. Using the same example of the pork loins, if the quotation is 90 cents per pound on 100 pounds of product and the buyer complains that this is too high, the price can be cut one cent for each 2 pounds that can be shorted and the dealer makes a larger profit.

In addition to items never delivered and the short weight, there is a third problem—quality. The club manager purchases a most perishable product—fresh food. The days when the manager personally selected meats and produce are mostly over, unfortunately. The complexities of the business preclude this. Usually produce is ordered sight unseen. Therefore, the first time that purchases can be inspected is upon arrival and in many instances buyers do not take advantage of this. When spoiled or under-quality merchandise is discovered it is difficult and time consuming to have the vendor make the proper adjustments.

A ready "check-off list" covers each item individually. This enables immediate discovery of any shortcomings and facilitates appropriate corrective measures.

Receiving Area

Every club must have a receiving area where merchandise can be properly accepted, and the orderly transfer from the vendor to the club may be effected. This may be a covered platform outside the kitchen area, a room with an outside entrance, a space in the rear-entrance corridor, or a space set aside in the kitchen. Providing such space does a number of things, all of which are important:

1. It establishes in everyone's mind that the club considers receiving very important.
2. The receiver does a better, uninterrupted job of checking and noting the delivery date on the purchase order.
3. It allows for the assembling and placement of the proper receiving equipment.
4. It limits the area that vendor's delivery men may use. A side benefit is that personnel designated to receive must then be physically present to accept the merchandise. The vendor's agent must never have unrestricted access to the kitchen.
5. It expedites the flow of merchandise into holding or working areas.

Receiving Personnel

Employees who do the receiving must be as carefully selected as the cashier who handles the cash. In this selection one cardinal rule must be rigidly enforced—the employee who receives must be someone other than the purchaser. In order to provide the basic internal control, purchasing must be separated from receiving. If at all possible, the receiver should not be given an opportunity to meet the vendor's salesman. Bonding companies report case after case where an employee who both purchases and receives has been subverted by vendors. This thievery takes many forms, but the usual are: (1) deliveries to the employee's home or a confederate's place of business, with the charge to his employer; or (2) kickbacks reflected in higher prices, short weight, or poorer quality than ordered.

The employee who does the receiving is designated as the storekeeper and has the responsibility for the safekeeping of the goods until they are ready for preparation in the kitchen. The easiest way to train this employee is to have all purchases written on a form with all of the details of quantity, quality, and delivery spelled out specifically. This form is known as a purchase order.

Receiving Equipment

The purpose of the equipment is to:

- more specifically designate the receiving area
- provide the tools necessary for the inspection of products; these should include, but not be limited to, a hammer, pinch bar, metal snips, and cardboard-case cutter.
- provide a scale for the weighing of products purchased by the pound; these are many and varied and they must meet the requirements for the particular business. If beef or other meat is purchased by the carcass, then a track scale is necessary and a scale graduated in ounces is needed. A bench type, or portable floor-dial scale is essential for most clubs and will weigh all other cuts of meats. A new scale recently introduced will print the weight of any product placed upon it on the purchase order, vendor's invoice, or on a strip of paper, simultaneously.
- provide a platform truck and a hand truck so that the merchandise may be quickly and economically moved from the receiving space to the holding area.

Receiving the Merchandise

The actual receipt of the merchanidse should always be systematized as much as possible so that personnel will adopt a set of routine procedures:

1. The storekeeper should be informed when the vendor's truck arrives. Unloading should never start until he is present. This prevents breadmen, milkmen, and others from entering the kitchen with their wares, and gives the storekeeper time to have his purchase order available at the receiving point, thus controlling the confusion when more than one truck is ready to unload at the same time.
2. The storekeeper will carefully check the merchandise against both the purchase order and the vendor's invoice (or at least one) for quantity and quality. All meats must be weighed and checked for quality and grade, with any variance from the documents noted. Dry stores, such as groceries, must be counted, and brand name and case size checked. Product must be inspected as to freshness, size, and in some instances weight. Equipment must be carefully checked

for shipping damage. A receipt for delivery will be given to the vendor's representative.

3. The weight or quantity (unit of purchase) will then be entered on the purchase order in the appropriate column. If a blanket purchase order is being used, the storekeeper will use the reverse side of the order to do the receiving. As merchandise is delivered he will fill in and complete the columns, retaining this document for the entire accounting period. He will forward only the vendor's invoices to the bookkeeper as the goods are received.

4. If the item received is club equipment, and a property and stock-record card is attached to the purchase order, the storekeeper will fill in the information on the card and forward it to the bookkeeper with a copy of the purchase order and the vendor's invoice (if available).

5. The goods must now be removed from the receiving space, refrigerated, or stored otherwise as required.

6. By means of a rubber stamp, the storekeeper will certify that the goods were received and found satisfactory on both the vendor's invoice and purchase order. Then he will sign and date the certification.

7. The storekeeper will retain one copy and forward the other copy of the regular purchase order and the vendor's invoice (if available) to the bookkeeper. A copy of the blanket purchase order will be forwarded at the end of the accounting period.

The manager who safeguards the "back-door money" by applying receiving techniques to his operation makes additional profits, removes temptation from his and the vendor's employees, and has the satisfaction of knowing that "he is in control of his club."

Issuing

In the club the custody of the food is usually assigned to the storekeeper or the chef. The best system of control is for all food to be received by the storekeeper in whose custody it should remain until it is transferred to the kitchen where it becomes the chef's responsibility. This transfer or the issuing of the food is a very important part of the overall food-department management.

The following principles should apply to all food moving from the storage areas to the kitchen:

1. The oldest stocks are used first. Good receiving practices demand that highly perishable items be dated for identification. Oldest stocks should be placed at the front of racks or shelves, with the fresh ones stacked at the rear.
2. Minimum quantities should be issued. To prevent waste and separation of holding areas, only the food necessary for immediate preparation should be issued. For frozen food the storekeeper controls the thawing cycle. Menus must control the variety of items issued and chefs must not "stockpile."
3. The food must be issued in usable quantities. To reduce waste the food package must be issued in the preparation size. If the kitchen uses sugar in five-pound quantities it will save money to issue it in five-pound lots. Sugar, coffee, flour, rice, and other items issued in bulk and stored in the kitchen have less than a 90 percent usage.

These principles apply to all methods of controlling the use of purchased foodstuffs.

Accountability of Food

On each delivery, clubs get a receipt and signature from the storekeeper. Thus if a receipt is given for all food that leaves his custody, he can be held responsible for the balance. Although this is the best system for food control, it is not practical for all operations. A small club cannot always afford a full-time store-keeper. A large club serving three meals a day with a varied menu may find it impractical to have a manned holding room for the twelve to eighteen hours the dining room is open. In these types of operations it may be necessary for some other person to have the responsibility for the food. One person, however, must be in charge of the security of the food to make sure that it is used for the purpose it was purchased.

Another problem area arises where a holding room is manned by more than one storekeeper. In this case, one man must be in charge with the authority to assume full responsibility for the food. If he feels that he cannot trust his subordinates he must take the necessary precautions to protect the inventory. These include spot checks, authority to hire and fire, and double-key control.

If the club operates with a storekeeper, the unmanned holding locations must always be kept locked. While on duty the storekeeper should always carry the keys to the locks. The keys should be left in the club when he or she is off duty.

Cost Control

So that management can ascertain the dollar value of the food, a system of control that can be applied to the food inventory is needed. These systems have four common ingredients. They must:

1. *Be practical and accurate*; as a system is developed it should be evaluated against the actual club figures. A good system should supply two facts: (1) the dollar value of the ending inventory, and (2) the dollar value of the food used. The total of these should be the value of the beginning food inventory plus all food purchases. Compare the figures from the cost controls with the actual financial statement figures. A variance of over two percent, without explanation, is cause for investigation.
2. *Give detailed information*; the system must be detailed enough so that the discrepancies, if any, are known and the responsibility for them can be pinpointed.
3. *Save money*; the system must not require labor or materials in excess of its value.
4. *Not interfere with kitchen routine;* bookkeeping and paper work assigned to kitchen food-preparation personnel is undesirable. Efficiency suffers when duties other than primary functions are assigned. One of the following systems should fulfill the particular needs of your club.

Storekeeper Issue Control System

This requires that the storeroom be manned, if not all the time the food department is operating, at least during breakout periods. All food is received into holding rooms by the store-keeper and issued to the chef using a triplicate, prenumbered

Requisition Form. The dollar value of the food on the form reduces the inventory by this amount and is the cost of the food. This amount subtracted from sales will determine the gross profit. When possible the requisition is prepared by the chef and signed in the "requisitioned by" block. This gives the chef an opportunity to ascertain whether any leftovers may be used, if condiments are needed, and to indicate the quantity of items desired. The storekeeper fills the orders and signs the "issued by" block. All signatures are dated. The storekeeper keeps one copy, as does the chef, and the original is forwarded to the office.

If an over-issue takes place this same form may be used to return items to holding areas.

Each item on the requisition is posted to the appropriate Stock Record Card so that a perpetual inventory record is maintained. The balance on the card is the amount of product in the holding area. If the cards and stock do not balance, one of the following nine things may be wrong:

- bulk goods were issued without accurate weighing
- goods were issued without writing out a requisition
- requisition not changed when items were not in stock
- inventories and requisitions priced wrong
- inventories counted wrong
- inventories and requisitions not extended
- spoilage not reported
- staff dishonest
- clerical errors in perpetual inventory records

Usage Inventory Control System

With this system, the chef is responsible for all food in the holding areas. Areas are kept locked and only he has the keys. Some person, usually the manager, maintains Bin Tally Cards for all products. The current quantity of the item and its last cost price are posted on these cards. As items are received and placed in the holding area, the additions are noted on the cards. Each time the exact food cost for the club is desired an inventory of used items is taken. When these are extended and added the total is the food cost.

Exhibit 5–3. Requisition Form

						NUMBER	

TO:

FROM:

Description	Unit	Quantity Desired	Quantity Issued	Unit Cost	Extension	Unit Retail Price	Extension

Requisitioned by	Date
Issued by	Date
Received by	Date

Part 1	Bookkeeper Copy
Part 2	Storeroom Copy
Part 3	Receiving Copy

Exhibit 5-4. Stock Record Card

| Reference | Date | Quantity | | Unit Price | Unit Reconciliation | | Total Balance | Valuation |
		In	Out		Unit Out	Unit Balance		

Manufacturer	Location			Retail Price	Optimum Stock Levels	High	Low
Description		Unit of Issue					

With this system, used for all items except bulk meat, inventory is taken and the quantity is posted on a card attached to the shelf where the item is held. For example, six on the card means six cans on the shelf. If there are five on the shelf at the next inventory, one can is posted on an inventory sheet and the tally card is changed. In almost all cases the work is reduced by recording what is missing rather than what is present. Items are added to the cards by a plus (+) sign so that the inventory taker can compute the necessary changes. Pin tags are used on bulk meats such as ribs and rounds. These are removed

Exhibit 5-5. Bin Tally Card

Date	Item	Size	On Hand	Cost Price Per Unit	High	Low

from the meat and are dropped in a box. The weight on the pin tags is then entered on the inventory sheets as "items used." Many clubs are using this system to establish daily control. It works well in any size operation.

Purchase-Order Inventory Control System

This is a system for the medium-size club. The chef has the keys to all holding areas and uses the products as needed. As soon as it is received the food is considered expended. The profit or loss, with the gross-profit percentage, is computed daily by adding up all purchases for the day and subtracting this figure from sales. An inventory of the food is taken weekly and the profit or loss is adjusted. If the inventory has increased, the additional profit is added. A decrease in inventory is subtracted from the profit.

Any one of these three control systems can be used for any-size club. An additional daily or weekly inventory on either a cost or retail basis may give all the information needed.

The system of inventory at retail works very well in a snack bar–type of food operation and for controlling certain kitchen

Exhibit 5-6. Purchase Order

	DATE	PURCHASE ORDER NO.
FROM:	TO:	DELIVER TO:

GENTLEMEN: Being governed by instructions hereon, please enter our order for the following:

Quantity	Description	Unit	Unit Price	Amount

Date Required	Discount Terms	Via	Signature of Authorized Personnel

Billing Instructions

A. Separate invoices must be rendered for each order.

B. Do not pack invoice with merchandise; mail under separate cover.

C. Transportation charge, when applicable, must be added to invoice.

D. Full name and address of this activity and PURCHASE ORDER NO. must appear on all documents accompanying, or have reference to delivery of this order.

NOTE: NONCOMPLIANCE WITH THESE INSTRUCTIONS WILL RESULT IN RETURN OF INVOICE AND DELAY PAYMENT.

NOTE: **NOTIFY US IMMEDIATELY IF UNABLE TO COMPLETE ORDER BY REQUIRED DATE.**

Part 1	Vendor Copy
Part 2	Bookkeeper Copy
Part 3	Receiving/Bookkeeper Copy
Part 4	Receiving–Retained Copy
Part 5	Purchasing Copy

items. The controlling factor is whether a retail value can be determined for every item sold. In a snack bar, presliced meats, prefabricated hamburgers, and other preportioned food items determine the retail value. For example, if ham is sliced for sandwiches and precosted portions are separated by wax paper, it can be controlled at its retail price. In precosting, all of the items used are considered including the bread, lettuce, tomato, onion, mayonnaise, etc., but for accounting purposes the meat is charged out at the total sandwich price.

If all items cannot be portioned and priced, another system of cost accounting must be used.

Another use of the retail system is for special events, when limited entree items can be inventoried before and after the event. For example, the club served a choice of a steak or lobster dinner on Sunday. The food was inventoried before and after the event and each steak and lobster missing represented one unit. The chef was required to have a sales ticket for each unit missing.

LABOR SAVINGS

The highest-priced labor is in the club kitchen. Therefore, any labor savings that involve the kitchen staff are worthwhile. There are many items that can be readied to reduce the kitchen labor.

1. Bulky vegetables can be washed and trimmed by the storekeeper. In some clubs this is done at time of delivery, thus reducing the holding space required.
2. All frozen items that must be defrosted before cooking can be issued thawed.
3. The storekeeper can save the kitchen valuable time if he works out a thawing cycle with the chef. All items can be thawed under refrigeration and before issue.

Vegetables

In general, frozen vegetables need not be thawed before cooking. However, there are exceptions—corn on the cob, greens, asparagus, and broccoli.

Corn should be thawed completely. The other items should be thawed enough to separate the leaves. If the package is opened in the vegetable reefer that is 31°F (−1°C) to 40°F (4°C), items will thaw completely in four hours. The storekeeper will issue vegetables to the cook ready to prepare.

Fruits

With the exception of melons all fruits are issued to the kitchen in a thawed state. Thawing will take five hours in the vegetable reefer if the package is open. Melons, (watermelon, cantaloupe, honey dew, etc.) will be thawed for only one hour under 31°F (−1°C) to 40°F (4°C) refrigeration and served immediately.

Meats

Most meats can be cooked—frozen or thawed. Thawed meat cooks more evenly, shrinks less, and stays juicier. With thawed meat, the chef can better judge the cooking time. Therefore, all meat, except steaks less than one-inch thick, will be issued in a thawed state. Steaks that are one-inch thick or less may be broiled thawed or frozen with no difference in evenness or juiciness. Usually the chef will prepare them frozen. They can be then left on the broiling rack longer, providing more time for the meal trimmings. Thickness, not weight, determines whether or not to thaw.

Seafood

Issue seafood thawed or frozen if it is to be heated; thawed if it is to be eaten without heating. To thaw under refrigeration allow eight to ten hours per pound. It is very dangerous to thaw seafood at room temperature because it spoils quickly.

In order for the club to have good issuing procedures it is necessary to train the personnel involved. Proper training must be part of the daily routine in every club.

PREPARATIONS

The manager who does not understand food preparation is sometimes taken advantage of by a skilled chef. The chef may be naturally arrogant, temperamental, and impervious to any criticism. These traits are always aggravated when the chef does not respect the manger's "food expertise." This in turn leads to management's fear that the chef may leave, as well as the possibility that menu selections, costs, and labor controls may deteriorate.

A fine chef is such a tremendous asset to a club that a manager should go to any lengths to obtain and retain this person. Yet, in every instance the manager must be the boss.

A meal can be produced without a chef. There may not be any tallow or sugar work, ice carvings, exotic dishes or sauces but the restaurant can operate if the manager understands something about food production. This has been done in some instances by teaching other employees, with only some cooking experience, to prepare the menu items from recipe cards. In discussing food preparation two other subsidiary items for management are (1) kitchens need not be miserable places to work in— they can be air conditioned, or have adequate air exchange and ventilating systems; and (2) the kitchen need not have a complete staff to open it. As business warrants, staff is added. The club is a business and can be run like one! With planning and organization, the kitchen can be made a very pleasant place in which to work.

The steps in the preparation of food will be discussed in the following order:

1. personnel
2. cooking
3. plating and distribution

PERSONNEL

The successful kitchen has recognized that each employee is an individual with different interests and motivations. Management

understands the capabilities, potentialities, and needs of each
person. Employees are continuously in training to advance to
better jobs. Promotions are always made from within the organization in the successful operation. If he takes advantage of
the tools available to him, the manager need not know how to
cook in order to supervise a kitchen with or without a chef.
These tools include standard detailed recipe cards, "how to
cook" books, and a pool of skilled labor available for training
and off-hour duty.

Although the kitchen staff will vary with the size and needs,
go slow in the hiring. Based on the following table, know when
there is a genuine need before additional persons are hired.

A comprehensive and consistent on-the-job training program
for kitchen personnel is necessary to insure that each person
understands his job and maintains a high standard of performance. A sharp organization can motivate an employee to do
formal and informal off-hour studying for advancement. Advancement from within is the greatest motivation for the employee's interest in the job ahead.

Table 5-1

	For 0 to 49 Patrons*	For 50 to 99 Patrons*	For 100 to 175 Patrons*	For 175 Plus Patrons*
Cooks	1	2	3	4
Salads				
Pantry	1	2	2	3
Baker		1	1	1
Dishwasher	1	2	3	3
Janitor				
Helper	1	1	1	1
Total	4	8	10	12

*NOTE: This table is for each meal served. It may necessitate more than
one employee for each job in a seven-day operation.

The club can obtain literature, slides, films, etc. for use in training. Information can be programmed as follows:

1. *Principles of Cooking* how to use recipes, food preparation, use of equipment and utensils, how to schedule work and make up a "Cook's Worksheet."
2. *Nutrition* nutritional value of various food, daily diet requirements, menu planning, and the importance of proper preparation to nutrition.
3. *Stowage* proper stowage procedures, care of holding rooms and refrigerators, keeping-qualities of foods in connection with and proper temperatures and humidity.
4. *Basic Arithmetic* developing skills necessary for figuring costs, selling prices, and recipes.
5. *Sanitation* importance of personal cleanliness, causes and prevention of food-borne diseases, proper care of food, equipment, utensils and work spaces, and pest and rodent control.
6. *Clerical Duties* proper procedures (and their purposes) for using the forms required to purchase, hold, issue, and account for provisions.

COOKING

All food preparation starts with the raw product in the raw-food processing or the salad-finishing areas. The food to be prepared is controlled by three factors: the menu, the recipes for the items of the menu, and the number of servings. Because the typical mean temperature of the kitchen, between 75°F (25°C) and 95°F (35°C), is ideal for harmful bacteria growth, food should never remain exposed for any length of time. Once the desired quantity of raw food has been initially prepared, it must be cooked. If it is salad or another cold item, it should be plated. The cook has a variety of cooking methods that will impart a different flavor to each end product. These include:

- baking or roasting by cooking in an oven
- braising cut-up fowl, rabbit, or veal; browning in a small amount of fat, a technique called fricasseeing

- broiling, as when heat is applied directly to the meat
- boiling in water
- frying in shallow or deep fat
- skewing chunks of meat on wooden or metal pins and cooking them
- stewing, a simmering in small quantities of liquid

In roasting, the cook may baste, barbecue, or marinate the meat to provide additional or different flavor.

Vegetables also may be cooked by baking, boiling, braising, frying, sautéing, scalloping, and steaming. Each method has its use and wide variation.

In the well-run kitchen, food is cooked for the customer, not the steam table. The table should only be used to hold food after the meal starts. Therefore, it is necessary for the inexperienced cook to have cooking charts so the proper starting times can be discovered, for items needing immediate preparation. Vegetables should be cooked in small increments to be served at their palatable best. The cook should remember that every vegetable (with the exception of whole potatoes, beets, and rutabagas) can be boiled in less than 30 minutes or pressure-cooked in the steamer in less than 10 minutes.

The two most common errors in vegetable preparation are burning and oversalting. If items are burned on the bottom, the cook should quickly dump the part that isn't stuck into another pan, add water, and complete the cooking. Adding water into a pan where items have been scorched only ruins the flavor of the unburned items.

Sometimes, oversalted food can be salvaged by adding a small quantity of sugar or vinegar, or both, cutting up some raw potatoes to absorb the excess salt or, if an item has no solid pieces such as soup or gravy, to increase the quantity.

PLATING AND DISTRIBUTION

The prepared food must now be placed on the vehicle that will carry it to the diner. Transporting the food on the plates the diner will actually be eating from is called Russian service.

English and French service calls for placing the food on platters or in serving dishes that are carried into the dining room.

If placed on a plate that is at room temperature and left to sit, properly prepared food can become unpalatably cold in just 5 minutes. Of course in a poorly ventilated or badly aired kitchen the time will vary, but the 5-minute figure is the one to work on! This can be extended in two ways:

1. preheating the plates
2. providing infrared or other warming units in the pick-up area; and using plate covers if the plates must be carried any distance

Modern equipment makes it easy to preheat plates. Many companies make a conveyor that contains a heating element. The conveyor is filled at the dishwashing machine cleaning side, wheeled to the cook's plate-preparation line, and plugged in to an electrical outlet. The cook can remove one plate at a time at any desired temperature.

When ready, the plate should be absolutely clean of meat grease or vegetable shreds. Each item should have a separate and distinct place on the plate. Any item that runs into another should be served on a separate side dish.

The eye appeal of any dish can be greatly enhanced by garnishes. Sometimes the cook overlooks the variety of ways a plate can be made more attractive. Listed below are a few ideas.

If the item is:

1. *Clear*—a thin slice of lemon sprinkled with parsley, a few slices of stuffed olives or slivers of cucumber pickle, a few tiny slivers of carrot for a color-contrasting orange, a few pieces of shredded, salted almonds
2. *Jellied*—chopped olives, watercress, mint, or parsley, slivers of pickle, sieved, hard-boiled eggs, slices of lemon
3. *Cream*—croutons, egg dumplings, diced cooked vegetables, pimento strips, grated cheese, a floating center island of salted whipped cream 2 inches in diameter, cooked, crisp bacon, shredded, salted almonds
4. *Heavy*—buttered popcorn, slices of smoked sausage or franks, diced crisp bacon.

5. *Fruit cups*—sprig of mint, green or red cherry, whole strawberry, small dip of ice cream or sherbert.

Other garnishing ideas for main-course plates are

1. *Seafood*—lemon slices or wedges, parsley, paprika, pimento, green pepper, radish slices, rolled anchovy fillets, capers, tomato slices topped with lemon, stuffed olives, celery and carrot strips, ripe and green olives, watercress
2. *Meat and poultry*—parsley, apple slices, lettuce and tomato, spiced peas, cucumber and celery strips, ripe and green olives, green pepper rings.
3. *Salads*—carrot curls, celery curls, cheese balls, cherry poinsettias, cucumber curls, green pepper rings, onion rings, pickle fans, radishes (plain and rosettes)

The distribution of the prepared food entails taking it from the kitchen to the consumer at its appetizing best. It is the cook's responsibility to ensure that when the plates are ready they are picked up by the waiter.

SERVING

In any club the most important person is the member. Regardless of the attractiveness of the dining room or the quality of the food, unless the service satisfies, it cannot be successful. The hostesses and waiters have more personal contacts with members each day than the manager has each month. Therefore, satisfactory service requires that the manager train, supervise, and motivate the dining room personnel.

The member considers himself to be closely associated with his club. He or she feels a certain personal embarrassment when service falters, and questions whether the club was a good dining choice. The club differs from a regular restaurant. In the restaurant a dissatisfied customer who makes a point of not returning nevertheless has little contact with the other patrons. In a club the disgruntled member has direct access to all of the clientele and can easily pass on that disgruntlement. Experience has shown that good service can overcome the handicaps of mediocre or poor food, poor decor, and home dining.

The serving of food is the broad title used to describe the entire dining-room operation and includes all factors of person-to-person membership relations. This relationship can be divided into the reception, "sale of menu", service to and departure of the member.

RECEPTION

The amount of work for the reception of the diner starts well before the diner's actual arrival. It is determined by the type and variety of the menu for that particular meal.

The manager should have a check-off list to evaluate the physical order of the rooms—the first element of reception. This can include the following:

Dining Room Set Up

Each table in the room should be set up with tablecloths or place mats and the proper silverware, glassware, chinaware, and linen for the meal. A room should never have excess tables that are left bare. If the room is too large, use room dividers or lounge furniture to decrease its size. This establishes an image of efficiency. It tells the member that the professional manager knows how many persons will be served and that service is prepared for them. A good figure to use is a 10 percent over-set. Seating should be varied to suit the needs with singles and dueces spaced along the perimeter with the fours, sixes, and eights in the middle of the room. Most fine clubs have switched to round tables for the sizes and eights. Round tables promote conversation between guests and create more of a club atmosphere.

The manager should mentally divide the room into waiters' stations and check for the service setups at each. The size of the club will dictate the number of stations. Each must be equipped to handle the members in that section of the room. The station has condiments, coffee cream, ice and tongs, glasses, ice water and pitchers, silverware, linen, butter in iced trays, coffee warmer, and serving pots. In addition the section should have sufficient tray racks to meet the waiters' needs.

The lighting must be checked to be sure that the club has the right atmosphere for the meal. If there are candles on the tables they should all be lit just before the room is opened. The ventilation and temperature must be checked for comfort. Carefully inspect the entrance for loose gear. Check the hostesses' station setup for menus, reservation forms, and general decor.

Preopening Employee Check

The manager should check with the person in charge of the dining room (hostess, maitre d', or head waiter) as to his or her knowledge of the menu being served. Information such as "what is the soup de jour," etc., can then be passed on to the serving staff. The waiter should inspect his station and the hostess should check the waiter. The waiter has certain housekeeping checks to make. These include:

1. *The cover*—Silverware should be clean and bright. Linen should be spotless and the napkin triple folded to the left of the fork. Cup and saucer, bread-and-butter plate, water goblet, and wine glass are usually on the table in addition to the silverware. In many clubs a service plate is used as a drink coaster and provides a nice touch. It is also practical as it dresses up the table and saves spotting the cloth. Salt, pepper, and sugar should be checked for cleanliness and adequacy. Flowers and candles should be arranged.

2. *The furniture*—The chair seat should be checked for dust and food particles, and should be wiped. The table base and legs should be checked for spots and blemishes. The rug should be inspected for foreign objects.

3. *The service sideboard*—Condiment bottles should be uncapped, wiped with a clean cloth, the top cleaned and then recapped. Cream pitchers should be checked and filled. A check-off list of the items stored here should be available to the waiter. This ensures that if necessary a complete replacement can be done prior to the dining room opening.

The hostess has the following responsibilities:

1. to check the overall physical appearance of the dining room
2. to inspect the service personnel's neatness and cleanliness
3. to relate the details of the menu to the service personnel
4. to distribute the dinner-guest checks to the waiters

When all these items are checked by the hostess and waiters, the dining room is ready for customers.

The hostess must greet each patron, ascertain the number of persons in the party, and conduct them to a table. The hostess is responsible for accurately distributing the work load in the dining room so that each station receives the number of diners in orderly rotation. She must also seat the party and present menus (if they are used). When the party has been seated the hostess departs by stating the waiter's name who will serve them.

SALE OF MENU

The waiter is essentially the salesman for your dining room. He should effectively complete the sale of delivering his merchandise to the member's satisfaction.

Management should train the waiter using these guidelines:

1. Encourage this service employee to study the menu and to ask the kitchen questions about the ingredients of the various dishes. As salesmen they must know the product in order to make a sale!
2. They should be told which items the house is especially proud of and which items are featured today. This gives the feeling that they are being taken behind the scenes and are members of the team. They help the undecided member make a selection by tactful suggestions.
3. They should be told to study the members and make appropriate suggestions, for example, hot soup for the tired and chilled; a salad for the overweight person.
4. Encourage them to take the wine correspondence courses so that they can make suggestions as to proper wines for a meal. In addition, where possible, a commision should be given for each bottle of wine.

5. They should be told that sincerity, friendliness, and good service help promote the club image in the member's mind.

6. Train personnel to check with the kitchen frequently so that they know when certain items run out.

7. Familiarize the personnel with the club advertising and bulletins so they can give the customer correct answers to questions about current and future activities.

TYPES OF SERVICE

Since there are various types of dining-room service, the manager must be acquainted with all of them. The type used should be that best suited for the club and each server must follow a predetermined specified procedure.

French Service

This is the most elaborate form of table service. The waiter/waitress serves the guests from a food wagon or side table. Before serving, attractive, tastefully arranged dishes of food are presented to the customers for inspection. The individual plates are then prepared by the waiter from the food on the platter, serving bowl, or chafing dish. In a modification of this service, the food is arranged on serving dishes, supplied with serving spoons and forks so the guests may help themselves. This is called "platter service." A single dish or the main course may be served in this fashion. In some restaurants the vegetables are served in this way. Others serve attractive, compartment trays of assorted relishes. Trays of assorted cookies are sometimes passed with an ice-cream dessert. French pastries are often offered to the customer on a tray.

Another variation of French service is the salad cart, now popular in some restaurants. Salads are placed on a cart and wheeled to tables where guest make their selections. The server prepares the salads on the cart and places them at each patron's cover. Another variation is to have prepared salads and desserts on the cart for the guest to select from.

English Service

This service is sometimes called "host service." When this service is used, the platters and serving dishes are placed before the host or hostess who serves the individual plates. The server stands to the right of the host, receives the prepared plate from him, and places it before each guest. Female guests may be served first, and then the male members of the party. However, the usual procedure is to serve each guest in turn, beginning with the person seated at the right of the server. This service is frequently used in clubs for private parties and should be available upon request. It could be used in serving teas at luncheons and birthday or anniversary celebrations. In each of these cases the club must have the necessary ware to make the event attractive. This service requires proper trays, platters, and cutting tools.

Russian Service

This is the service in which the entree, vegetables and garnishing are placed on a plate in the kitchen, carried into the dining room, and served. This type of service was originated, for formal dinners, by Czar Alexander of Russia in the early 19th century as a direct slap at the French court for its "pièces montées." These were great constructions of edibles that were wheeled into the banquet chambers where the guest would be served. This service is the most frequently used in clubs today.

American Service

This is a combination service between different traditional styles. If, for example, the appetizers are selected from a tray, the main course is brought from the kitchen already plated and the host cuts and serves a cake for dessert. In short, the best of the three types of service are used to fit individual needs.

Buffet Service

With this style of service, the guests help themselves from a table set up with a variety of attractive foods. The buffet table can be used for the entire meal or just for certain courses, such as salads, appetizers, or desserts. If the guest is to serve himself he should be given a large buffet plate (12 inches) on which he places the food he selects. The server should serve soup, breads, and beverages at the table as it is very hazardous for guests to walk around carrying these items. A tray should not be used or it will become a cafeteria and the elegance of dining will be lost. When hot food is served, there should be servers at the buffet table to carve the roast, serve vegetables and the other foods from casseroles, chafing dishes, and platters.

A "smorgasbord" is the name given to a buffet style that originated in Sweden, offering a great variety of items. A large selection of typically Swedish items such as appetizers, relishes, smoked meats, fish, and salads are arranged on the table. Sometimes this buffet includes separate tables displaying varieties of fancy desserts.

In normal club table service, after the member has been given the menu by the hostess, the server should approach the table, fill the water goblets, and inquire if the guests would like to order cocktails.

The member must be allowed to place the dinner order at his convenience. He may wish to relax with a cocktail before he makes his selection. In any event, the patron must not be hurried—he must be allowed to set the pace. As the order is written, details of preparation (such as rare steaks, etc.) should be asked for and noted. The server than asks whether the group desires separate checks.

After recording the member's order on the guest check, the server may suggest a bottle of wine with the meal. This must be a gentle, easy sell such as "Did you notice that we are featuring 'Wine with Dinner' this week?" If a bottle of wine is ordered, it should be served immediately, unless the waiter is advised of the serving time by the member. This will please the customer as well as create the possibility of selling a second bottle.

There are certain general service rules that management should train waiters to follow. These are:

1. Bring all food from the kitchen on a tray.
2. Serve and remove all beverages, including water, from the right of the guest.

3. Use the left hand to place and remove dishes when working at the left side of the guest, and the right hand when working at the right of the guest. This avoids bumping the member's arm.

4. Present serving dishes from the left side when the guests serve themselves. Place serving silver on the right side of the dish, with the handle turned toward the guest, so that he may reach and handle it easily.

5. Never reach in front of the guest, or across one person in order to serve another.

6. Place each dish on the table with the four fingers of the hand under the lower edge and the thumb on the upper edge.

7. Check to see that the guest is not using soiled, chipped, or cracked glassware or china, bent or tarnished silverware.

8. Hold silverware by the handles when it is laid in place; be sure it is clean and spotless.

9. Do not lift water glasses from the table to fill or refill. They can be moved to a more convenient location on the cover, if necessary.

10. Use an undercover for juice and cocktail glasses, soup bowls and dessert dishes. They should be placed in the center of the cover between the knife and fork.

11. Place the salad, when it accompanies the main course, to the left of the forks about 2 inches from the edge of the table. When the salad is served as a separate course, place it directly in the center of the cover.

12. Place individual serving trays of bread and rolls above and to the left of the forks. Place bread for the use of several guests toward the center of the table.

13. Place the cup and saucer to the right of the spoons, about 2 inches from the edge of the table. Turn the handle of the cup to the right, parallel to the edge of the table.

14. Set tea and coffee pots on small plates and place them above and slightly to the right of the beverage cup. Set iced beverages on small plates or coasters.

15. Place individual creamers, syrup pitchers, and lemon plates above and to the right of the cup and saucer.

16. Place milk in a glass to the right of and below the water glass.

17. Serve all items such as butter chips, cheese, etc. with a fork or a spoon.

18. Always remove the soiled dishes of one course before serving the next, and crumb the table as needed.

19. When serving members in a booth, two of the general service rules may have to be modified by these suggestions:

- Serve everything with the hand farthest from the guest; use right hand to serve a guest at your left hand and left hand to serve a guest at your right.
- Remove soiled dishes with the hand nearest your guest while substituting the next course with the hand farthest from the customer.

DEPARTURE

Departure is treated as a separate part of food service to emphasize its importance.

The guest should not be kept waiting for his check. It should be presented immediately after the guest has made his last purchase.

The check should be accurately totaled and laid face down on the table to the right of the cover of the host. If the host is not known and the party has indicated one check, it should be placed in the center of the table. When a man and woman are dining together the man is given the check. The member should be thanked when the check is presented.

It is a courteous practice to mention the denomination of the money given to the waiter and to return the change on a small tray with at least some silver. Where tipping is permitted the change will encourage the customer to leave a gratuity. The waiter should remove the tray, look at the customer, and say "thank you."

Guests should be shown small courtesies when departing. Instruct servers to move back chairs, and assist with wraps if needed. The maitre d' should thank the members and express the hope that they enjoyed their meal.

SALES CONTROL

The controlling of sales in the food department is essential in forecasting preparation, making menu changes as needed, and accounting for money.

One method of control is to mark a copy of the menu with each item sold. This is maintained by the cashier–food checker (these jobs should be combined wherever possible) and after each meal, the menu can be analyzed by the management. A chart can be used to determine the popularity of each item offered and menu changes can be made as necessary. All items tending to overage before use must be eliminated. This "popularity" chart is also necessary for pricing individual items because it is sometimes virtually impossible to get the desired markup on each item. Clubs, for example, may find they cannot markup a high-priced steak to yield, say, 55 percent gross profit, or the selling price would be too high for its clientele. However, the chart may show that some lower cost items are, as a group, as popular as steak and can be moved up in price without hurting sales. This factor can be used to adjust prices.

The position of food cashier and checker should be combined. In a club with regular table service, a food cashier who is not working in a spot positioned between the food and the diner can only collect for those items listed on the guest check. When an a la carte–style menu is used many items could be deliberately or carelessly missed. A food checker may also check for uniform portions, proper garnishing, and insuring food is served at the proper temperature.

In controlling the sales money, one basic principle seems to work without exception: have at least two people involved in the transaction, neither of whom is the customer. This is handled differently for types of service involved. A fine control system for this regular service can be built around the prenumbered duplicate guest check distributed by the food checker. After the customer's order is written, the waiter leaves the original with the food checker and gives the duplicate to the chef. The server takes all food to the diner via the checker so that the tray can be scrutinized and each item on it checked. The chef uses the copy as a receipt for the food ordered and, at the end of the shift, seals the copies in an envelope provided, forwarding them to the office. The server gets the completed, original check from the checker when the member is ready to pay, and presents it to him. The money and the original are sent back to the checker who collects the records and cash. A daily-activity report is prepared and the documents and the cash are forwarded to the office. The checks from the chef can be compared with those from the cashier and control maintained. The bookkeeper maintains a check-off list of the guest checks to be sure all of them come into the office.

To combine buffet and table service, the member is given the duplicate if he chooses to buy the buffet. This check is surrendered to the employee on the serving line who in turn gives the duplicate to the chef. At the end of the meal the chef forwards the checks to the office. The server retains the original and submits it, with the member's money, to the checker.

If the service is exclusively buffet or smorgasbord then tickets or guest checks may be used as long as they are sold by one person and collected by another.

Cafeteria-style service is controlled by trying to have two employees in the line, one as a checker and one as a cashier. If this is not possible have the cash register turned so that the ring-up is visible to a food server, preferably one who is acting in a supervisory capacity.

The point to emphasize in all food control is that the member can never satisfactorily become involved in it; the manager must depend on the club employee.

In summing up the food business in clubs, one thing is apparent—it is an operation of a thousand-and-one details. From the planning of the menu through purchasing, receiving, storing, issuing, preparing, serving, and selling, management must play an important role. Personal attention and supervision never stops in the really well-managed club.

GOLF

The management of the golf course is not highly technical, but the maintenance is. Managers must have a competent greens keeper who fully understands the properties of the grasses. If a green is "lost" (cannot be played upon) the expense of replacing it could take an entire year's profits. The manager's job should include working with the golf committee to establish rules necessary to protect the course. In this respect, the manager should be interested in the following:

The danger of damage to the golf course can be substantially reduced with a "golf cart road."

1. Is the course being professionally maintained?
2. Are the members happy with the condition of the course, the golf professional, the pro shop, the equipment carts, flags, etc. and the locker room?
3. Have the starters been trained to make the game easier and more fun for the members?
4. Are records being maintained for all types of lessons being conducted?
5. Has the golf committee considered incorporating any modern developments in course utilization? These include:

   - starting on both the front and back nine
   - five-somes
   - penalty for play over four hours
   - a four-hour club
   - filling in some sand traps
   - fairway marked in fifty yard increments starting at 150 yards out and ending 50 yards from fairway
   - scorecard with time for each hole

Professional maintenance of club golf carts prolongs their normal life expectancy by about 80 percent.

6. Are incomes and expenses within the budgeted figures?
7. Are women getting a fair share of the starting times?
8. Are the playing rules being rigidly enforced?

By opening and getting satisfactory answers to these questions, the manager is assured success.

TENNIS

As the club needs a golf professional so it also needs a tennis professional. If there is to be a successful tennis division, the manager should be primarily interested in the following:

1. Is the maintenance of the courts on a par with the rest of the club? Are the nets whole and stanchions intact and erect, are the screens and backstops intact? Are the courts swept promptly when rain stops? Are the lights clean?
2. Are the members happy with the condition of the courts, the tennis pro, the pro shop, the equipment, and the locker room?

The tennis pro is encouraged to provide group as well as individual lessons.

3. Has a good social and competitive program been developed?
4. Is a good court-reservation system in effect?
5. Are tournaments well planned and managed?
6. Are accurate records being maintained for all types of lessons?

SWIMMING

The manager depends on the senior lifeguard for the day-to-day operation of the pool. The manager must know the danagers of this recreational activity so that safe practices will be implemented and supervised.

Managers should concern themselves with these particulars:

- The apron around the pool is usually very slippery and if horseplay is allowed invariably there will be falls.
- Diving boards must be securely anchored.
- Sliding boards must have both width and depth of water at the end of the slide to avoid injuries.

The popularity of tennis prompted many clubs to light courts for night play.

- The water itself must be checked continually when crowds use the pool to gauge the effectiveness of the chemical additives.
- Alert and well-trained life-guards are a must.

In addition the manager must be aware of the members' feelings about the pool. They must be happy with its operation. Swimming lessons should be provided, competitions arranged, and an all-around aquatic program should be maintained. The poolside furniture must be attractive and clean.

VENDING MACHINES

The manager has three options in operating vending machines:

Two club pools, one for adults only and one for families, will please everyone.

1. A contract can be negotiated with a concessionaire to install and service the machines. The club is paid a percentage of all sales made. The contracts are usually of one or two years' duration and the club's take is usually from 35 to 50 percent with no investment and no expenses. In the long run, this has proven to be the most profitable method of operation.
2. The club may purchase and stock its own machines.
3. The club may rent machines from a concessionaire and stock the machines with its own personal stock.

The club may even have a combination with some machines supplied by a concessionaire and some club-owned or operated.

If the first option is selected the manager should have a set time each week for the machines to be harvested and stocked, except in the event of malfunction, when the machine should be repaired as soon as possible. By advance scheduling the manager should have a club employee accompany the concessionaire to witness the servicing machines.

REVIEW QUESTIONS

1. Discuss the research necessary to do proper labor planning, and detail the items on the weekly schedule.
2. Discuss the concept of the kitchen being a manufacturing plant and the labor-saving devices that can be used.
3. Discuss the two methods of allocating general and administrative expenses in operating departments and what the value is of this concept.
4. Discuss the techniques of good buying practices and explain how each applies to the club.
5. Discuss the reasons for using "purchase orders" and the ways that they help in merchandise control.
6. Discuss the "built-in" security that a club might initiate to provide protection for its merchandise.
7. Discuss the basic concepts of cost control as applied to the food department.
8. Discuss dining-room guest reception and the training that may be necessary.
9. Discuss the manager's need-to-know operational knowledge of the golf, tennis, and pool departments.

6

Accounting

and Cost Control

OVERVIEW

The aims of this chapter are to explain fully the support systems department and the various systems necessary to establish control of the internal workings of the club.

The functions of the support systems department including bookkeeping, cost accounting, and systems implementing are fully detailed. The systems needed are schematically described so that installation of any of them can be accomplished if necessary.

These systems include the control of consumable merchandise, supplies, labor, and overhead. Energy is discussed and efficient usage is stressed.

RESPONSIBILITY

The support systems department has the responsibility for providing the accounting and cost controls for the club. Under the comptroller the principle functions are bookkeeping, accounts receivable, and cost controls. The methods used in handling these tasks are varied, and can be fully- or semiautomated, or done by hand. The volume of business will determine the method. These are:

- Have a computer at the club, prepare the material, and produce the required data.
- Rent time on a computer.
- Contract for a computer company to message and produce the data.
- Use a bookkeeping machine.
- Post by hand.

These functions, as with all actions of the support systems department, are confidential and should be revealed only to authorized personnel.

Bookkeeping

The manager must understand that the books of the club are a record of its financial history and the events depicted are already past. However, there is some truth in the adage that "history is prologue," and the club books as historical prologue are useful in many ways. The manager, however, needs to know the mechanics of club bookkeeping.

Posting

Whether the bookkeeping tasks are performed manually or mechanically the first function is to post the documents of the club into one of five journals. These documents are:

Daily Activity Report (DAR)—This report is prepared by the operator of each cash register and is a record of the sales made for a particular period. The period is usually determined by the availability of someone in the bookkeeping department to read the register and remove the tape. The report lists:

- cash sales
- charge sales
- change fund
- over and under cash register rings

- unusual happenings at the location of the register that should be recorded; these could be accidents to members or employees, visible drunkenness, etc.

Attached to the report are the guest checks and the charge slips for either in-house charging or credit card. For example the guest check would be used for in-house charging. But if the club were using credit cards then a copy of these charges would be forwarded. Then the report, the money, and other documents are forwarded to the central cashier via a hopper-type safe. The cashier removes and verifies the money, prepares a bank deposit slip, and sends it to the bank. The Daily Activity Report, and all the sales slips then go to the bookkeeper. The bookkeeper removes the charge slips after verifying the total and gives these to the accounts-receivable clerk. Then a member of the bookkeeping department goes to the register indicated at the top of the Daily Activity Report, unlocks it, reads and removes the cash-register tape. The bookkeeper matches the amount shown on the tape with that recorded on the Daily Activity Report. Cash discrepancies are noted on the Daily Activity Report and on a form called "Cashier's Over and Short Report" (see Exhibit 6-2).

Petty Cash Vouchers—These are the forms used to transfer funds in-house to an employee so that a cash purchase can be made. They should be prepared and controlled by the central cashier. The vouchers contain such information as:

- who received the money
- what voucher is for
- who received the purchase
- a vendor's invoice or sales slip

The voucher and all documentation is accumulated until such time as the funds need to be replenished at which time they are totaled and a check is drawn to reimburse the fund. The cashier presents the vouchers and check to the manager who insures that the vouchers are stamped "paid" and dated to prevent re-use. They are then delivered to the bookkeeper.

Purchase Order (PO)—The purchasing agent prepares a

Exhibit 6-1. Daily Activity Record

			Register No.
Name of Department		Signature of Cashier	Date

	Item No.	Item	Amount
Lines 1 thru 6 to be filled in by cashier	1.	Cash Turned in (Detail Below Item 20)	$
	2.	Change Fund (−) (When Turned In With Receipts)	
	3.	Refunds (+)	
	4.	Cash Sales	
	5.	Charge Sales	
	6.	**Total Sales**	$
Person verifying cash and charges will verify lines 1, 2, and 5 and fill in lines 7 thru 11	7.	Change Fund	
	8.	Cash Receipts	
	9.	Total Cash Verified (Line 7 + 8 = 9)	
	10.	Charge Sales	
	11.	**Total Verified (Line 9 + 10 = 11)**	$
Person reading the register will fill in lines 13 thru 18	12.	Closing Register Reading	
	13.	Opening Register Reading	
	14.	Register Amount (Line 12 − 13 = 14)	
	15.	Over-Rings (−) and Under-Rings (+)	
	16.	Refunds (+) (To Be Used When Refunds Are Reflected in Regular Register Readings	
	17.	Adjusted Register Reading (Line 14 ± 15 + 16 = 17)	
	18.	**Cash Overages or Shortages** (Circle: Overage or Shortage)	$

19. Breakdown of Revenue
(To Be Filled In By Bookkeeper)

Name of Account	Account No.	Debit Amount	Credit Amount
Total		$	$

Signed Refund Vouchers Will Be Attached
REMARKS: (Use reverse side if necessary)

20. Detail of Cash Turned In
(To Be Filled In By Cashier)

		Amount
Coins	Cents $	
	Nickels	
	Dimes	
	Quarters	
	Half-Dollars	
	Total Coins	$
Currency	One's	
	Five's	
	Ten's	
	Twenty's	
	Total Currency	
Checks/M.O.'S	U.S. Checks	
	Other Checks	
	Money Orders	
	Total Checks/M.O.'s	$
	Grand Total Cash Turned In	$

Signature of Person Designated to Read Register	Signature of Person Designated to Verify Cash and Charges

Note: To Make Corrections: Line through error. Write correct amount above error. Initial and date. Corrections are made only by person making error. <u>No</u> corrections will be made to lines 1 through 6.

Exhibit 6-2 . Cashier's Over and Short Report For the Month of ____

Date	Cashier's* Name		Cashier's Name		Cashier's Name		Cashier's Name		Cashier's Name	
	Over	Short	Over	Short	Over	Short	Over	Short	Over	Short
1										
2										
3										
4										
5										
6										
7										
8										
9										
10										
11										
12										
13										
14										
15										
16										
17										
18										
19										
20										
21										
22										
23										
24										
25										
26										
27										
28										
29										
30										
31										

*Note: Each employee who handles club funds (bartender, clerk, cashier, etc.) is
        listed.

Purchase Order for every item that is bought, with the exception of those purchased with petty cash. At least a four-part form is used with one copy to the vendor, two copies to the storekeeper, and one copy to the bookkeeper. The bookkeeper's copy establishes a contingent liability for the club. This allows the bookkeeper time to sort out and flag those vendors who give a discount for prompt payment. A ½- to 2-percent discount on purchases could completely refurbish a club department over a period of time.

The storekeeper, using the regular Purchase Order, will mark one of the copies "received and found satisfactory" and forward it with the vendor's invoices (if any) to the bookkeeper. On some shipments the invoices may be mailed separately from the merchandise. If the vendor does not furnish two copies of the invoice the duplicate must be made in the office. The storekeeper's copy of the Purchase Order with the vendor's invoice is checked against the copy the bookkeeper received from purchasing to see that prices and quantities have not been changed. The original Purchase Order is filed in the vendor's file so that the purchasing agent has ready access to it. The spare copy of the vendor's invoice goes to the cost-control clerk and the rest of the documents go into the file for the monthly business.

Club Requisitions—A record is made of all movement of merchandise within the club by use of a "requisition." Prepared in triplicate, this form records any goods moved from the holding rooms to an operating department, or back to the holding room, or from one operating department to another. For example, a requisition would be prepared for

- food moved from the holding room to the kitchen
- tomato juice, eggs, and oranges moved from the kitchen to the bar

The storekeeper uses one copy as the receipt for merchandise issued and forwards the other two to the bookkeeper. One is retained, the other given to the cost-control clerk. The dollar value of the merchandise on the requisition is the cost of the merchandise used.

Inventories—The inventories of each activity are prepared

by the bookkeeping department, priced and forwarded to the operating department. The quantities of items on hand would be entered and the forms returned to bookkeeping.

Time and Payroll Records—The employee time-records, including forms for any type of leave granted the employee, are collected by the payroll section of the bookkeeping division. Very few clubs compute and draw checks for a payroll as most major banks can economically handle these transactions, including making all federal and state reports.

Other reports that might come into bookkeeping are:

- cashier's report on accounts
- vending-machine reports
- members dues and assessment reports

Journals—The bookkeeper posts the documents in one of five journals. If the bookkeeping is mechanized, then a card or a tape is punched, and the information is fed into a computer—but the results are the same. These journals are:

1. *Cash Receipts and Sales* All sales both cash and charge are posted as well as all cash flowing into the club from any source.
2. *Purchase* All purchases and their payments are posted here.
3. *Stock Control* By adding purchases to existing inventory totals and subtracting requisitions, the dollar value of the inventory can always be determined. This is called the "book value" and is balanced against the physical count of the inventory.
4. *Payroll* If the club is handling its own payroll this journal is necessary; otherwise entries are made into the general journal.
5. *General* This is the catch-all where entries are made when they do not fit into the other four. Examples of such entries would be:

   - items for which the club must compute or estimate charges such as the employer's share of FICA, or the utilities if the club's closing date and meter reading are not synchronized.
   - adjustments to members accounts; these could be due to club errors or write-offs due to death, etc.
   - adjustments to club accounts to balance inventories, etc.

Also the general journal is used to close the journals of the club and enter the totals into the club's ledger accounts.

Ledger—The ledger of the club has a sheet for every account in the journals and usually runs from two to five hundred pages or ledger entries. The book is divided into two parts: the balance sheet accounts, and the profit and loss sheet accounts. The balance sheet accounts are those that run from month to month such as cash, inventories, accounts receivable, etc. The Profit & Loss accounts indicate the income and expenses for one month and then are closed out so fresh accumulations can begin.

Trial Balance Sheet—When the ledger is completely posted, the totals are entered on a sheet of columned paper into two columns. These columns are totaled. If they are equal the books are in balance.

Financial Statement—The financial statement for the club is prepared from the journals, the ledger, and the trial balance, and will reflect the profit or loss for a particular period within the fiscal year to date, showing all balances of the clubs assets and liabilities.

Cost Accounting

The support department accumulates all of the documents necessary to do the cost accounting for the club. It is the manager's responsibility to establish procedures so that these documents are prepared and forwarded.

The objectives of cost accounting are:

1. Safeguard the merchandise of the club. The system starts when the goods are received and ends when the employee gets the cash or credit card for them.
2. Safeguard the cash of the club. The system starts with the members handing cash or credit cards to club employees. It ends when the money is deposited and the credit sales are paid for.
3. Curb payroll abuses and to pay only for work performed.
4. Give management exact and detailed information on problem areas in the club so that corrective action can be taken.
5. Give management exact and detailed information so that decisions concerning selling prices, services, recreation and entertainment can be arrived at.

Practices

Every transaction in the club must be exactly defined and leave an "audit trail." This means that in the event of problems an exact path had been staked out for the employee to follow and footprints will clearly show where the employee left the path. For example, at the end of an accounting period the book-value inventory was $678 more than the physical one. This means the inventory is short $678. The storekeeper may read this disclosure in these ways:

- Keep the holding areas locked at all times and restrict egress of all personnel as much as possible.
- Carefully check every item on the PO for quality, weight, and price before signing for it.
- Make sure that every item leaving the holding area is recorded on the requisition.

The documents that make up the "audit trail" are:

- the beginning inventory
- the purchase orders
- the requisitions
- the guest checks
- the closing inventory

In checking the items on the beginning inventory it is found that the club had 1500 pounds of choice, trimmed ribs of beef on hand; 7800 pounds was purchased during this accounting period for a total of 9300 pounds to be accounted for; ribs of beef on the requisitions totaled 8100 pounds, while the ending inventory shows 600 pounds in stock. This means that 600 pounds at $1.13 per pound are unaccounted for. Management would then determine whether they were used by the club or stolen. The documents for this branch of the "audit trail" are the guest checks. The beef used in accordance with the inventory was 8700 pounds. The receipt for a roast rib dinner calls for a one pound serving (raw weight) per customer. The items of ribs on the guest checks should total 8700. If they do then the club had requisition or posting errors. If the guest checks however, total less portions sold, the club knows that it must carefully check its procedures and security.

Cost-control systems are very expensive in labor and have no value whatsoever unless management acts on the information provided. Fortunately however, management usually finds that the club used the goods and the storekeeper just forgot to mark them down.

Control Systems

The very best and most economical control system is called "Budget Control System." It is the basis for all other systems performance. This system treats every operating department as a separate business with its own complete overhead as explained in "Planning the Service Offered" in Chapter 5. Too many clubs with systems based on departmental gross and net expenses and profit wind up in the red because of overhead. The question answered for management by the Budget Control System is what percentage of the total overhead should each operating department share. To initiate the control systems the management starts with the food division. This is the most difficult to control and usually is the source of the greatest financial losses.

Food Division Control

The permanent control will be by the Budget Control System (BCS) method. This system is predicated on management's having accurate data on which to base the operation. The control steps that will be taken are as follows:

1. Accumulate the food-division overhead-cost data.
2. Establish recipes, portions, and selling prices for all items.
3. Establish the "Storekeeper Requisition System." This is only a temporary expedient until management is satisfied that the chef is trained and other responsible personnel are felt worthy to hold security keys. In very small clubs this step could be skipped in light of office calculations using guest checks and inventories. Inventories are taken by portions as well as by weight; inventories

are then balanced against the guest checks. Using ribs of beef again as an example, in slow-cooking methods a 15-ounce raw rib yields a 12-ounce serving. If 200 pounds were on hand at the beginning inventory, this would be shown as 213 portions. Added to this would be any further purchases, and subtracted from it would be the ending inventory. The chef is responsible for the missing portions which should balance with the quantity sold as indicated by the guest checks. The drawback to this procedure is that only the entrees are counted while all other ingredients costs of the meal are only known after taking inventory. In a small club the system works, however.

4. Establish the exact labor cost of preparing and serving food.
5. Establish the food checker and guest check system.
6. Take weekly inventories until the actual food cost is within 2 percent of that budgeted. Then take monthly inventories.

Once these systems are established and working, the division is run solely on the Budget Control System. The paper work in the kitchen is reduced to:

- the chef's supply list that goes to the purchasing agent
- the guest checks forwarded to the bookkeeper after every meal

Management now has only the problem of insuring that all items purchased are received into the club, and making all foods the chef's responsibility. There will still have to be locked storage for supplies, renewals and replacements, and for other divisions of the club such as the bar and shops. The keys, however, should be the responsibility of the department managers.

Recipe, Portion, and Selling-Price Control

The first control the manager installs should be uniform recipes and portions. The chef will transmit all recipes used in a written form and a loose-leaf notebook will be used to store them. The notebook of course is to be made available to any cook, coming in handy if the chef becomes ill or goes on vacation. The portions to be served will be specified, becoming part of the recipe. The prices charged, unless absolutely ridiculous, should not be changed until the entire system has been established and is working.

The selling price of each menu item is computed to check the percentage of food cost. The raw cost of each item will be subtracted from the selling price. This is the gross profit. Gross-provided divided by sales indicates the gross-profit percent. Gross-profit percent subtracted from 100 equals the percent of cost-of-goods-sold. For example, a typical menu item may be a steak dinner for $4.95:

12-ounce "Western Choice Sirloin Steak"	2.00
1 salad	.14
1 baked potato	.10
sour cream, chives, butter	.04
bread and butter	.04
1 beverage	.10
Total cost	2.42
Gross profit	2.53
Gross profit percent	51%
Cost of goods sold percent	49%

Different menu items may return different percents of profit. Therefore a scatter sheet will be used to determine what the overall profit should be. This is computed by the same method used to compute member usage of the club. For example:

10% of the items sold yields 51% gross profit
50% of the items sold yields 49% gross profit
30% of the items sold yields 48% gross profit
10% of the items sold yields 45% gross profit

This sales mix would yield 48.5 percent gross profit and is arrived at by multiplying the percent of product sold by the gross-profit percent adding them and dividing by 100 percent. This procedure is necessary in order to analyze the gross profit percentage on the financial statement which only shows the total of all items sold. The 48.5 percent figure thus is the forecast that can be compared to the actual.

Storekeeper-Requisition Control System

As explained in the bookkeeping paragraph this system will control inventories. However, to work, the system needs full-time storekeepers and cost-control clerks. Each item listed by the storekeeper must be posted on a stock card, maintained by the clerk, and subtracted from the previous total. In the food department the dollar value of the items can be the cost of the food used that day. However, in a large club there is so much error-prone paper work involved that this system is only recommended as the second step in the BCS.

Management should get directly involved in the requisitioning of food for at least a thirty-day period. This means that the manager and any other supervisory personnel will actually work with and in some cases in lieu of, the storekeeper. A very careful check of all food requisitioned should be maintained. That which is not used should go back into holding with the appropriate entry made on the form.

The purpose of this exercise is to train the chef in food usage and make it very clear to all personnel that management is vitally interested in the operation of the kitchen.

Labor-Cost Control

Labor-cost control starts with a broad overview of the job that is to be done. This overview is called a "job description," and each club employee should have one. A detailed "job analysis" should follow. This tells how to do the job. The "job description" (for blue collar workers) or "position description" will name the tasks the job encompasses. The manager need not bother however, to write the descriptions as CMAA has published a book entitled *Position Descriptions for Clubs.* The analysis will be written on site. As the employee must also be trained, the job analysis lends invaluable help.

After the employee knows what is expected in the way of job performance the controls really begin. Job control has three components.

1. Approved work schedule—The composition and need for the schedule is fully explained in Chapter 5.
2. Employees time record—The employee must sign in and out using either a manual or mechanical method. A sheet of paper with the employees listed by name and space provided for the days and the hours of work will suffice, or a time clock may be used. A permanent record of the employee's services is a very important document.

3. Supervisor's certification—Each time-sheet entree or card must be signed by the employee's supervisor to certify that the employee worked the hours specified on the work schedule. Employees are paid the scheduled time or the actual time worked, whichever is the lesser. This prevents employees from reporting in earlier or staying later than needed. All overtime must be approved in advance by the manager or assistant and noted on the work schedule if the employee is to be paid for it. This advance approval could be heeded even for the five minutes before an employee is scheduled to leave; making this a firm policy usually saves the club money.

Food Checker and Guest Checks

Quality control is as important in a club as merchandise and cash control. With planning, all three can be tracked by one person—the food checker. To work this system all the dining room tables are numbered.

Location—The food checker must be located just inside or just outside the entrance to the dining room. Usually a kitchen is planned with a pantry either between the kitchen and the dining room or as a room off the kitchen but readily accessible for the service staff. The pantry holds appetizers (shrimp cocktails, etc.) soup tureens, salads, hot and cold drinks, bread, rolls, and butter, all condiments including salad dressings, and desserts. Service personnel are trained to prepare these for the customer themselves; but only the club food checker knows whether or not the member pays for them.

If the food checker must be in the dining room, the stand with the cash register should be screened off.

Guest checks—The system starts with the bookkeeper issuing the numbered, triplicate guest checks to the checker. The checker is supplied with a change fund, a priced menu, and a list of the service personnel who will be working this shift. Guest checks are issued by the checker to the waiters/waitresses in increments of ten and the numbers are recorded on the service personnel list. The waiter/waitress takes the member's order by writing it on the check and including the table number. The original and one copy are left with the checker, as the stand is passed, and a copy is given to the chef or person behind the plating area. Under this system all food leaving either the kitchen or pantry area can be checked for quality and quantity. It also insures that it is recorded on the guest check as the service person gives the table number to the checker and presents the tray in passing.

The great saving given by this system is on impulse buying and desserts. In a party of four, two persons decide they want appetizers. When they are presented, one of the other guests now wants one. The checker must record it immediately.

Desserts rarely appear on the original check and without a checker the club must rely on a busy service person remembering to write them down. Even beverage and multiple dessert carts can be controlled by holding the carts at the check stand and having them served by the pantry person. When the member is ready for the check it is totaled and rung up on the register. The original is given to the waiter/waitress to be presented to the customer, and the copy is retained until the money or charge slip is received. The original is retained and the copy given back to be returned to the member with the change or the member's credit card.

The checker now records the guest check on a spread sheet that lists the menu items, the guest check total, and, if a tip is included on the check, the tip amount along with the service person's name.

At the end of the shift a DAR is prepared and is dropped into the depository safe along with the money, all charges, guest checks, and spread sheet .

Budget-Control System (BCS)

Once food, supplies, labor costs, and overhead have been determined the club can work in the weekly inventories of food and supplies used to establish further control. The requisition and payroll systems establish exact costs. By dividing them with sales, percentages are established. The profit or loss of the food division can then be determined. For example:

Sales	100%
Less	
Food Cost	50%
Labor Cost	35%
Laundry	3%
Supplies	3%

Renewals and Replacements	2%	
Overhead	12%	
Total Cost of Goods Sold and Expenses		105%
Loss		5%

*Note: Supplies are a one-time usage item such as paper goods, soap powder, etc. Renewals and Replacements are still an expense but they have some life expectancy. These are the glassware, chinaware, silverware, table linens and small kitchen tools.

Now management has figures that are accurate and can be used for decision making. The manager with the board of directors or their committee representatives can decide if a 5-percent loss is satisfactory. The manager will convert this to dollars. For example, on $250,000 worth of food business this represents $12,500. Can this amount be allocated to the division in terms of club dues? If not, the manager can offer the following options:

- Raise prices and/or eliminate losses.
- Cut service by closing during unprofitable periods; consolidating dining areas; eliminating the frills, flowers on tables, expensive table china, glassware, silverware and linen.

The division would be stabilized at whatever figure was decided and then management would use the BCS for its daily operations. This is a form of "risk management" that allows for a food cost variation to budgeted goals. This variance is the cost of establishing a control system. For example if a club had a 50 percent food cost on $250,000 in sales, the cost of food will be $125,000. The percent of variance would be calculated on the $125,000 figure. One percent would be $1250, this is the risk factor. If a system involving a storekeeper and cost clerk was established the cost could be justified by the risk involved. "Risk management" also dictates that total sales and total expenses be within 2 percent of the budget. This is determined by weekly inventories. If the figures stay within prescribed limits for four consecutive weeks, the inventories are taken every two weeks. If after four weeks the club is still within limits, a once-a-month inventory is sufficient. If either exceeds these percentages the club immediately reestablishes complete control steps.

The club budget is a method of forecasting the income and expenses in each department. By using cost of goods sold and expenses as percentages of sales, variances from forecasted to actual can be immediately spotted.

If for example, the budget indicates the projected cost of goods sold is 50 percent, the labor cost 35 percent, and other expenses, both direct and indirect, 20 percent, the forecast indicates a 5 percent loss. If the actual loss is 5 percent then management knows that it has absolute control of its resources. This can be seen in Exhibit 6-3.

Snack Bar Control

A club's snack-bar food-and-beverage operation can be controlled by Budget-Control System or a system called "Retail Accountability." The Retail Accountability system establishes a retail value for every item sold with the inventories and purchases figured at both cost and retail. For example, the beginning inventory in the snack bar, added to all purchases, less the ending inventory (if figured at the selling price) should equal sales. The Retail Accountability System requires that every item sold be prepackaged in the club kitchen and transferred to the snack bar by requisition. This is costly in manpower and the Buget-Control System will work equally as well if deliveries can be arranged so that the vendors sales slips and the club purchase orders separate the snack-bar food, beverages, and supplies from those of the kitchen.

Buffet Control

The control of the cost of goods sold on buffets and the money it generates is not complicated but requires a great deal of research to start. The control of the goods is accomplished as follows:

Exhibit 6-3. Bar Inventory by Retail Accountability Method

PAGE_____OF_____

Stock No.	Item	Unit	Beg Inv	Issues	Sub Total	End Inv	Amt Used	Unit Cost	Total Cost	Sell Price	Total Price
	Michelob Draft Beer	Lb.						.141		.333	
	Schlitz Draft Beer	Lb.						.117		.267	
	Michelob Beer	Btl.						.204		.45	
	Schlitz Beer	Can						.16		.30	
	Schaefer Beer	Can						.131		.25	
	Schmidts Beer	Btl						.115		.25	
	Colt "45"	Can						.158		.30	
	Corn Chips	Pkg						.071		.10	
	Beernuts	Pkg						.071		.10	
	Potato Chips	Pkg						.071		.10	
	Slim Jims	Ea.						.105		.15	
	Beef Jerky	Pkg						.105		.15	

Retail Accountability		Cost Analysis		Responsibility	
Expected Income		Sales Per Register		Bartender	
Sales Per Register		Total Cost		Inv. By	
Short/Over		Gross Profit		Calculated by	
		Gross Profit %			

Remarks:_____

1. A menu for the buffet is planned. This can be supplemented by leftovers but these constitute only a small part of the total.
2. Every item must be weighed and priced, exactly as is done for an individual meal.
3. When the meal is over and the buffet broken down, every item that is still salable must be weighed, subtracted from the beginning list, and returned to stock.
4. The total sales figure is divided into the cost figure, and gross profit is computed.
5. The gross profit is adjusted by:

   - increasing or decreasing the variety of items; the greater the variety the higher the cost. If there are twenty-five items weighing 100 pounds this would feed 100 persons. However if thirty items are put out weighing 100 pounds this will not feed 100 persons.
   - having less or more expensive items on the table
   - raising or lowering the price charged

The control of the money is as follows:

1. If the buffet is the only choice offered, have the checker sell the guest checks at the front desk and have them picked up on the buffet line by a responsible person. A stub on the check could be given the member for identification when getting a second serving.
2. If a regular menu is offered in addition to the buffet, use the normal method and have the service personnel write up the guest check at the table.

In either type of meal served the member is always escorted to the table, seated, served water, and invited to order cocktails or wine.

Private-Party Control

A private party is any affair arranged by a member or customer where the participation is limited and one person or a group of persons is financially responsible for the costs. The manager in order to have absolute control must:

- have a contract with the host
- have a list of menu items available with prices and portions figured. These menus would include

Hor d'oeuvres selections. These are usually light, medium and heavy and are priced by the person. For example: one club serves the following for $1.00, 2.00 and 3.00 per person respectively, for groups of twenty-five or more persons.

Light hors d'oeurves

Chips and dip   Peanuts
Deviled Eggs   Stuffed celery

Medium hors d'oeurves

All of the above plus
Raised puffs of tuna and chicken
Assorted cheese trays   BBQ meatballs
                Shrimp eggroll

Heavy hors d'oeurves

All of the above plus
Fruit boat
Baron of Beef carved at the table with hot biscuits, butter, mayonnaise and mustard.

In addition the club offers hors d'oeurves by the tray. The trays contain 100 pieces and would usually feed about thirty-five persons. These come in both hot and cold foods and some selections offered are

Hot hors d'oeurves

Mini drum sticks   Teriyaki beef
Shrimp puffs   Pizza rolls
Cocktail franks   Fried shrimp
Breaded mushrooms   Rumaki'
Cheese sticks   Miniature tacos

Cold hors d'oeurves

Cold cut platters   Pastrami
Sliced roast beef   Corned beef
Sliced ham   Tuna salad
Shrimp salad   Chicken salad
Sliced chicken   Sliced turkey
Lox and cream cheese   Gelatin salads
Cold slaw   Potato salad
Pickles, olives, cauliflower, etc.

- prepare breakfasts, brunches, luncheons, and dinners that can be served to a group, usually priced on a per-person basis.
- provide wine and other alcoholic beverages—wine is priced by the bottle, beer by the glass, bottle, pitcher or barrel, hard liquors by the drink, bottle, or person; if drinks are sold by the person the club should set a time limit on the party; figuring four-and-a-half drinks per person the first hour, three drinks the second and third, and two drinks per hour from then on.
- have a diagram of the club rooms available for the party and draw in the seating arrangements; if music is to be supplied indicate where the orchestra will be set up and whether or not there will be dancing.
- discuss and write down all details of the party such as:

flower arrangement	cloak-room attendant
special equipment (projectors, video, sound, microphones, etc.)	candelabra
	blackboard and chalk
	imprinted matches
musical instruments (piano)	guest book
podium	special food (wedding or
spot lights	birthday cakes, etc.)
flags	ice carving
red carpet for reception lines	cigars, cigarettes and after-
doorman and valet parking	dinner cordials

- discuss and record the following financial arrangements:

When can the club expect payment?
How much is the gratuity to the staff?
Should the club require a deposit and a guaranteed number of persons?

Beverage-Cost Control

The control of beverages, particularly alcohol, offer a special challenge to the club manager. The very nature of the product itself tends to promote mischief and wrong-doing. It is of little wonder then that controlling these products is almost as difficult as food-product control—but for different reasons.

When the product is manufactured and sold by the same person, it is difficult to get two persons involved in the transaction. Many methods have been tried, with varying degrees of success, to get the member served involved. These are:

1. Prepare a guest check for each transaction and prering the check on a cash register as each drink is sold. This looks good but the bartender can underring or not ring up a drink at all in order to increase the tip. Even in clubs, it has been observed that the member doesn't care.
2. Have the cash register built into the bar so that it is possible for the member to observe whether or not the drink was rung up.
3. Use the "Red Star System." This was devised by a cash register manufacturing company to sell machines that printed a receipt. This receipt comes from a roll within the register and red stars spaced at irregular intervals throughout the roll have been printed on it. If the member's receipt contains one of the red stars his drink is free, the purpose being to involve the member in the transaction, hence safeguarding the club.

   Unlike the kitchen where the chef observes the complete operation, the bar manager may have operations going on in every part of the club. Where the portions on a plate are clearly visible to the food checker, the bartender can under- or over-pour with no quality of quantity control of the product. Also on a busy bar it may be very difficult to establish responsibility for the money or inventory.

   Bartenders work alone much of the time; therefore a "drinking habit" may not be detected if the employee is discreet.

Control Steps

In spite of the problems outlined above, the bar can be controlled and, as in the food division, there are definite, necessary steps management must take.

1. Accummulate the division overhead-cost data.
2. Establish standard drink portions, brands, and recipes.
3. If at all possible hire inexperienced personnel to tend bar.
4. Use the requisition system to transfer beverages from the holding room to the various bars.
5. Establish complete bar stations for each bartender.
6. Establish the labor costs for the division.

7. Install retail accountability and daily inventories at retail, until a track record is established for every bartender.

Once these steps have been established and are working, the bar is now solely on the BCS of requisitions and monthly inventories, if the actual cost is within 2 percent of the budgeted cost.

Standard Drink Portions, Brands, and Recipes. The portions of alcoholic beverages served in each drink is set by the management. The size is determined by:

- the desires of the membership and their willingness to pay
- the size of the glassware used; a 1-ounce drink in a 10-ounce glass may be too light, whereas one-and-a-half ounces in a 4-ounce glass may be too strong. Clubs generally pour one and a quarter or one and a half ounces in a 6-ounce highball glass. If the member desires a lighter drink then an 8-ounce glass is used. The member would order a "scotch and water tall" to get the lighter drink.
- a shot glass (jigger) or an automatic system; if a jigger is used about one third of the beverage comes from the glass and two-thirds free pouring. This is accomplished by training the bartender to tilt the jigger over the glass at a 45-degree angle. Pour into the shot glass until it runs over, and continue to pour from the bottle for two seconds. In training, the count is one, two, three without pause.

It is proper for clubs to have very fine products in the well. This reduces inventory, speeds up drink production, and helps create a "club atmosphere." The purchasing agent should determine the brands by using the "best-sellers list" that every distributor has. The club should also have a back bar of the finest products from around the world.

The recipes must be standardized for every bar and every bartender. This is the only way management can be sure that the member will always get the same drink, in the same proportions, and mixed the same way.

The manager soon learns that there is no "right way" to mix any drink, unless an invention of the club. Therefore, a good book of alcoholic recipes must be purchased with the drinks the club will serve compiled into a handbook for every bartender. It is necessary to be selective in preparing the handbook or it will not be used. Allowance should be made, however, for as wide a variety as possible to cover all personal preferences a club member might have.

Hire Inexperienced Bartenders. The most difficult job for any manager is training the staff. The second most difficult job is untraining them. It is virtually impossible to teach an experienced bartender who trained himself to "do it the club's way" if he has always done it differently. Habits that are hard to break are:

- drinking behind the bar
- picking up the ice and drink garnishments with hands
- not closing the cash register drawer after each sale
- not using a jigger
- not smiling at the customer
- eating behind the bar
- sloppy mixing and serving
- not washing hands frequently
- being unkempt in personal appearance
- smoking behind the bar
- no interest in the club's schedule; a good bartender will know the operating hours of every department in the club.
- more interested in TV than in the members

For these and many more reasons, managers have found it was much easier to teach the inexperienced than untrain the old bartender. Training is a slow but easy process if the manager hires a presentable man or woman and lets the membership help. The manager informs the membership that an inexperienced bartender is keeping bar and after introducing the novice to various members, will suggest members be open about giving the bartender helpful instructions.

Use the Requisition System. The same procedures are followed in the bar as in the food department. Start with issuing the stock needed to the bar manager indicating to which of the bars the merchandise is going.

Establish Bar Stations. A bar station is a space behind the bar that is completely self-supporting. It contains all the stock that the bartender needs, all the supplies, ice, and a cash register either for money or guest-check imprintment or both. By this method, the bar manager can pinpoint responsibility and establish a track record for every bartender.

As the bar will be controlled by a system called retail accountability the only separation of items in ringing the cash register will be items shared with another station. For example, if the club uses an older remote-draw system for its draft beer two or more stations may share it and the beer should be represented by a separate cash-register key. The new remote systems measure the beer with a flow-meter which can be installed in existing systems.

When there is product sharing of this inventory by two or more bartenders, a separate cash-register key will only tell the manager that the product use and cash amount do not match and that he has a problem. The only solution for this problem is personal observation. This can be done by management or by any of the firms that specialize in "shopping service." This service provides for a company representative to "shop" the bar by buying one or more drinks and providing a very comprehensive report to the management. The "shopper" is usually provided with a guest card to authenticate his or her presence.

Establish Labor Costs. The manager will establish the labor costs for the entire division including the bar manager, all bartenders, all service personnel, all buspeople, and any other labor used to serve beverages.

Retail Accountability

The system of retail accountability in the beverage division means keeping track of all product by its retail value. For example a fifth of bourbon (750 ml) would produce, at .90 cents a 1½-ounce shot (45 ml), 16½ drinks with a dollar value of $14.40 (16½ × .90). The ½ ounce (15 ml) is lost in capillary attraction, spillage, etc.

The system is designed so that management, through inventories and issues, can determine the least amount of money the bartender should have recorded. Inventories of a bar are taken in tenths with the use of a bar scale and are calculated at both cost and retail value. For example, the selling price of an item would include the cost of mixes and garnishments—a gin and tonic would be priced by establishing the price of

45 ml of gin
120 ml of tonic water
¼ of a whole lime

Then actual cost divided by percent of cost will equal the selling price. The gin, tonic water, and lime cost 18 cents and a gross profit of 75 percent in the bar would satisfy the BCS requirements. The cost-of-goods-sold percentage is 100 percent minus the gross-profit percentage, or 25 percent. Therefore:

$$\frac{\text{Actual cost}}{\text{Percent of cost}} = \text{selling price}$$

$$\frac{.23}{25\%} = 92 \text{¢, raised to .95 or \$1.00.}$$

However, in computing retail accountability, if the average selling price of 45 ml of gin is 90 cents then the inventory calculation would be 90 cents. The system uses the lowest or most conservative price the bottle will return as the amount on which to base the bartender's responsibility. Managers should use a standard chart, available from the brewery, to compute the number of glasses of beer that can be drawn from the barrel. Beer barrel is a misnomer as the steel keg used by all breweries is not a barrel but a half barrel. It contains 58.67 liters of beer (15.5 gal.); the old beer barrel contained 117.35 liters. If the beer is drawn correctly the number of glasses drawn cannot be determined by dividing the size of the glass into the amount of beer in the half barrel as the foam or head on the beer is 75 percent air.

Inventories should be taken daily for the first thirty days of the installation of the system. If actual sales were within 2 percent under or 5 percent over the estimated sales, weekly inventories should be taken for the next thirty days. Then inventory in the third month should be taken in the middle and at the end, using the Budget Control System as the control yardstick. Twice a month inventories should be taken at least for six months before the bars are put on a once-a-month inventory since the control data must be accumulated at least for this length of time.

Happy Hours or Reduced Prices

In some clubs it has become customary to have reduced prices in the bar at certain times as a promotion gimmick. This is simple to control if all prices are reduced approximately by the same percentage. The cash-register tapes are marked at the beginning and at the end of happy hour. For example if all drinks were reduced 50 percent from 5 P.M. to 7 P.M. for all sales during this period, for computation purposes 50 percent would be added back to check the accountability.

Regular sales	190.00	4 to 5 P.M.
Reduced drinks	80.00	5 to 7 P.M.
Regular sales	300.00	7 to 11 P.M.
Total sales	570.00	
Adjusted by 50%	80.00	
Inventory check	$650.00	
Product used	645 (less than 5% over)	

This indicates that the bar was operating satisfactorily. If sales are reduced by any percentage, subtract this from 100 to set up the percentage of what is added to the actual sales for an inventory check. For example, all drinks are reduced 35 percent. Subtract 35 percent from 100 percent and the result is 65 percent. Then: 35% ÷ 65% = 53.8% which would be added to the actual sales for inventory check.

Regular sales	$490.00 for the evening
Reduced drinks	80.00
Total sales	570.00
Adjusted by 53.8%	42.96
Inventory check	$612.96

Another method of control is to use a separate bar for reduced-price drinks with a pre- and ending inventory.

EXHIBIT 6-4 Departmental Budget

Department: _____

		1	2	3	4	5	6	7	8
		Oct	Nov	Dec	First Quarter Budgeted	First Quarter Actual	Jan	Feb	Mar
1	Revenue								
2									
3	Cost of Goods Sold								
4									
5	Gross Profit								
6	% of Sales								
7									
8	Direct Expense								
9									
10	Wages and Meals								
11	Salaries and Wages								
12	Employee Meals								
13	Total Wages and Meals								
14	% of Sales								
15									
16	Other Direct Expense								
17	Supplies								
18	Renewals and Replacements								
19	Repairs and Maintenance								
20	Laundry								
21	Misc. Direct Expense								
22	Total Other Direct Expense								
23									
24	Total Direct Expense								
25									
26	Direct Activity Profit (Loss)								
27	% of Sales								

9	10	11	12	13	14	15	16	17	18	19	20	
Second Quarter Budgeted	Second Quarter Actual	Apr	May	Jun	Third Quarter Budgeted	Third Quarter Actual	Jul	Aug	Sep	Fourth Quarter Budgeted	Fourth Quarter Actual	
												1
												2
												3
												4
												5
												6
												7
												8
												9
												10
												11
												12
												13
												14
												15
												16
												17
												18
												19
												20
												21
												22
												23
												24
												25
												26
												27

ENERGY

The club must not pay for energy that is nonproductive. If a piece of equipment is turned on and not needed for production, if a space is lighted and not used, if a space is heated or air-conditioned and no one occupies it, the club is wasting money. This is a serious consideration. But, of equal importance, the club is also wasting precious energy. Whether or not there is a real energy crisis makes no difference. The government and energy suppliers say there is and allow energy prices and products to reflect this stand-making another financial drain for the club manager.

Club House Energy Program

The club energy program can effectively be based on common sense around the possible and the practical. Here is a check list of items for management to keep in mind:

1. Keep the club house as close to 68 degrees as possible when the heat is on and the building is occupied, and 60 degrees at all other times.

2. Keep the building as close to 68 degrees as possible when the air-conditioning is on. Humidity control is a direct part of air-conditioning. Have an expert check to see that the system is balanced. Do not raise the temperature when the building is unoccupied, unless you are closing down for a week or more.

3. All outside lights, including those in the parking lot, must be on "shadow switches." These will automatically turn the lights on and off as needed.

4. Have automatic door-closers on all doors.

5. Run continual usage checks against all outdoor or satellite recreation areas. Make recommendations to the board on whether or not to continue their availability when they have to be lighted, heated, or air conditioned.

6. If the pool is heated by gas, oil, or electricity, check the availability, installation expense, and upkeep of solar heat.

7. Consider modifying a golf cart with a small pick-up body for short trips around the club area. There is approximately a 50-percent savings over a standard gasoline truck.

8. Give the maintenance department the responsibility for a scheduled check of:

- windows and skylights
- doors (including equipment doors) such as on ovens and refrigerators
- heating and air-conditioning equipment
- air-handling equipment and duct work
- prime movers such as motors, engines, and turbines
- fans and pumps
- hot and chilled water, and steam piping

Kitchen Energy Program

The biggest user of energy in the club is the kitchen. A constant watch is required to operate this space and the equipment in a sensible manner. Management can take these steps to conserve energy.

1. Turn off infrared food warmers when no food is being warmed.
2. Inspect refrigeration condensers routinely to insure that they have sufficient air circulation and that dust is cleaned off coils.
3. Train employees in conservation of hot water. Supervise their performance and provide additional instruction and supervision as necessary.
4. Avoid using hot or warm water for dish scraping.
5. Keep refrigeration coils free of frost build-up.
6. Reduce temperature or turn off frying tables and coffee urns during off-peak periods.
7. Preheat ovens only for baked goods. Discourage chefs from preheating any sooner than necessary.
8. Run dishwasher only when it is filled.
9. Cook with lids in place on pots and pans. It can cut heat requirements in half.
10. Thaw frozen foods in refrigerated compartments.
11. Fans that cool workers should be directed so they do not cool cooking equipment.
12. Consider using microwave ovens for thawing and fast-food preparation whenever they can serve to reduce power requirements.

R E V I E W   Q U E S T I O N S

1. Discuss the various responsibilities of the support department.
2. Discuss the method the bookkeeper used to accumulate data in preparing the monthly financial statement.
3. Discuss the objectives of the cost accounting system.
4. Discuss the method of determining the selling price of the meals and drinks served by the club. Detail the factor involved in presenting a food department budget to the board of directors.
5. Discuss the usage and need for a system to control labor.
6. Discuss the control steps necessary to establish a system of retail accountability.
7. Discuss the methods the manager can use to conserve energy.
8. Compute the selling price to gross 55 percent profit if the dinner food ingredients cost $1.73.
9. Compute the cost of the food ingredients of a dinner that sold for $6.95 and grossed 51 percent.
10. What gross profit would a sales mix yield if the following were calculated?

   12% of the items sold yield 61%
   18% of the items sold yield 54%
   30% of the items sold yield 49%
   40% of the items sold yield 45%

7

Advertising

OVERVIEW

The aim of this chapter is to acquaint the student and manager with advertising concepts. These include the methods and procedures that are necessary to keep the club interesting and alive, to attract new members, and keep the present ones.

Some of the things to avoid are also discussed and the relationships between advertising, promotion, and merchandising are explored.

Methods for advertising each segment of the club are given detailed attention.

ADVERTISING THE CLUB

Club advertising is the responsibility of every member and every employee, and one of the manager's important duties is to insure that everyone understands this. The formula is simple in its statement—employee-created enthusiastic members equals more members—but is so difficult in its execution.

Time and time again stories are told about advertising—businesses that are spending hundreds of dollars on advertising while losing customers when just a few extra thoughts spent could have kept them. The first step in advertising, though, is getting a product worthy of publicity.

When the club is ready to advertise the manager will prepare with the finance committee an advertising budget for submission to the board of directors. This budget could be in three parts: part one, the program to attract new members; part two, the publicity to entice the members to use the facilities; and part three, information on club activities.

ATTRACTING NEW MEMBERS

Whether or not attracting new members will be part of the advertising program depends on the type of club being managed. Many membership clubs have a waiting list. Any advertising would be an affront to those persons on the list. However, in most commercial-type clubs, new members are actively sought.

In developing the program the manager would consider these steps:

Exclusiveness—In the club business, there is some merchandising viability in exclusiveness. Snob-appeal has always had some affect on certain people and could be an important factor. The advertising must be very low key. A nice brochure, in color, should be available for pickup in the club or for members to mail to friends. A stamped envelope with the club's return address completes the package. Never include an application for membership in any piece.

Facilities—Which of the many club facilities need to be advertised? Are the links filled to capacity but the courts, pool, and dining room in need of members? If a facility could use additional business, stress this. In speaking of facilities, be honest. If adjectives such as "championship," "beautiful," "challenging," "gourmet," "fabulous," etc. are used, make sure that they understate the activity. Always mention if the pools are heated and lighted, courts air-conditioned and lighted, the driving ranges or putting greens are lighted. Mention any facilities not normally offered by other clubs in the neighborhood.

Equipment—If there is anything exceptional or unique in the club's equipment or service, emphasize it, especially such things as:

Games

- repair facilities
- storage facilities
- mobile bar service on the links, courts, and pools
- wind shields on the courts, and pools
- sauna and/or steam rooms
- party and banquet facilities for members
- stock-market ticker
- children and teenage programs
- baby-sitting
- giant-screen television
- unique wine cellar
- bicycle facilities—paths, storage, and repairs

People—continually build up the reputation of the club's professionals. Besides the athletic ones, remember the chef, master bartender, maitre d'hotel, repairmen, assistant managers, bilingual employees, and other persons with talent.

Club History—If the land, buildings, or locality have any unique historical significance, emphasize this in advertising.

INCREASING MEMBERS' UTILIZATION OF THE CLUB

The manager should never take for granted the fact that members know all about the facilities, equipment, and people in the club. As frequently as twice a year, a brochure (prepared for new members) should be included in the envelope with the members' bill.

The following additional communications and sales methods could also be used.

Party Brochure

Create a printed party brochure listing all the services the club could furnish for:

- weddings
- birthdays
- anniversaries
- celebrations of any kind
- special events

Emphasize the professionalism the club has available to *stage* these events. Use the word "stage" frequently in the pamphlet. Use color for the pages or print, and use 8 × 8-inch paper so that when folded the brochure will be 4 × 8 inches. Mail these to the entire membership at least annually with a monthly bill. If a club brochure was mailed in January and June then the party brochure could be mailed with the August bills to take advantage of the holiday season.

Feature the ease of entertaining at the club, the service, the unique menus available including a complete gourmet dinner.

Posters

These should never be used for announcements as this wastes time and money. The manager considers posters as advertising, he is "selling" not announcing. In preparing the message to be communicated, written words and pictures must yield the correct "sales appeal." A poster is never complete without a picture so plan to have photos or graphics available for each one. In designing posters consider the following:

1. It must stop the member long enough to be read.
2. Spotlight the poster either with overhead lighting or from the rear. A cutout poster with translucent letters and pictures can be very effective.
3. Vary the size. The available poster board is limited in size. Use half of one or two, three or four full sheets. Mix the colors.
4. Vary the language, print, and spelling. A Mexican night at the club could be advertised in Spanish. Members stop to translate it to each other. A poster in "Olde English" might be different (an Italian dinner offered in Latin is unusual.) Using misspelled words as an attention getter can sometimes be effective, at least causing comments.

Flyers

"Flyers" are single-sheet advertising for a single event. A single sheet of paper has information printed on it about a party—the cost is low and distribution can be widespread. It is unparalleled for simple effectiveness. Have the flyers available at the club's front counter, on cocktail tables, and at the bar. Consider newsboy delivery as well as mail delivery to member's homes. Also don't forget cars in the club parking lot.

Menu Clip-Ons and Table Tents

A small, attractive card, clipped to the menus, both in the dining room and cocktail lounge, is a very effective advertising method for special events. A table tent (a folded card resembling an open-ended tent) is a little more expensive, as both sides must be printed, but is more effective.

INFORMATION FOR MEMBERS

Information for all members is provided by means of a monthly Club Bulletin. This piece should contain advertising even though it is concerned both with past events as well as coming ones. In planning the club bulletin, don't overlook these items of interest—winners of tournaments with pictures, unusual scores in any sport or game, attendance at special parties, etc.

Appearance—Each monthly bulletin must appear different from the preceding month. This is done by changing size, shape, color, and format.

- Size   Use miniature or oversize to vary the 8 X 10-inch format or 8½ X 11-inch the printer will suggest.
- Shape   Use shaped bulletins for variety. Also consider different folds.

Content—The manager keeps in mind the purpose of the bulletin, which is to advertise and inform. The advertising is easy if the members are interested in seeing their names in print, with their picture or friends' pictures. Some ways to develop and hold this readability follow:

1. Print a picture of one officer, director, or committee chairman each month. If possible use an action shot.
2. Print action shots of members. Pictures of individual members are never printed more than once a year unless the member wins the club championship twice or has accomplished some other newsworthy feat.
3. In an alphabetical file keep every name published, whether in text or picture caption, and try to balance the pictures, half and half, women and men.
4. Print a picture of an outstanding employee about four times a year.

Every party planned should be publicized in the bulletin. If the manager requests permission the first few times, members will accept and look forward to the fact that the details of their party will be in the bulletin. Printing a monthly day-to-day calendar in blocks and filling them in does not improve readability. A block is attention-getting; thirty blocks are boring. A list in which the more important complete-membership events are listed will be read. Management will insure that every private party is printed up with the same style and imprint of type used. It is too much to expect that every member will open the bulletin and read every line of it. However, the manager can increase the chances of readability by spotlighting items that management particularly wants the members to read, "boxing" them. This means putting them in a space by themselves and surrounding them with an outline. In spite of the title, "boxing," squares should not be used. Use circles, colors, and varying widths for attention-getting. Also English reading habits are to be kept in mind. The prime space on any sheet is in the exact center with the other spaces being, in order of preference, upper-lefthand corner, lower-lefthand corner, upper-righthand corner, lower-righthand corner, upper middle, and finally lower middle. This also applies when preparing poster, flyers or menus.

"Brag a little" in the bulletin, as long as it is based on fact. The manager is always striving to make both the membership and employees proud of the club. Tell the members about the new idea you had, the new employee or piece of equipment that is going to serve them, or anything else that applies to them.

THE MENU

In planning menus the club manager has an opportunity to mold the character of the establishment, direct the efforts of the employees, provide the best utilization of equipment, and affect the net profit or loss for the club.

It does not seem to make any difference whether the menu is printed or oral, written on a blackboard on the wall or presented on glazed cardboard, as long as the fundamentals of preparation and presentation are observed.

It is possible to have a poor operation with a good menu but it is impossible to have a good operation with a poor menu!

Using the menu to create an attractive image is sometimes overlooked by planners. Everyone is aware of the harm that can be done by menus that are soiled, or unimaginative, that require too much preparation time or equipment, deliberately falsify the product, and present it poorly. Still the value of proper menu planning is nevertheless underrated.

The club manager must first know that, through menus, the character of the establishment can be affected, thus creating a "public image," and then plan to take advantage of it through every means available.

The factors involved in creating the desired image are:

1. type of customer
2. location of dining room
3. type of dining area
4. hours of service

These factors will determine the material on which the menu is planned and the method of presentation to the member. The planner will separate the members into two broad categories: 1) those who are present for some other purpose than to partake of food, and 2) those primarily interested in eating. In the first group are the members using the swimming pool, bowling alley, golf course, or snack bars, the bingo-intermission snack, etc. Also in this group are members who attend special entertainment functions such as dinner theatres, etc. In the second are members partaking of the main dining room meals of breakfast, lunch, and dinner and including those sponsoring the special group functions. In regards to the special group function always have a menu on the table for sit-down serving. There is no menu choice, of course, as the food details have been determined in advance, but the menu can stimulate the members taste-buds and advertise the club. Members often take these menus home as souvenirs (which they should be encouraged to do) and use them in planning future functions!

Athletic Menus—These are best presented on a bulletin or blackboard, on or behind the counter, and function when either counter or waiter service, or both, are used. This eliminates the use of a menu that would be handled by a member with wet or soiled hands, allows for last-minute changes to meet weather or inventory changes, and creates an informal atmosphere.

Special Entertainment Menus—This menu must be very limited, usually of three courses: entree, salad, and beverage. As the attention of the member is on the entertainment only a few interruptions should be allowed. To illustrate: Present a two-night bill of "Ten Nights in a Barroom" starting at 8:30 P.M. in the main dining room. The regular dinner is served until 8 P.M. Then as the show starts, baskets of pretzels are placed on the tables and beer (sold by the pitcher) and other drinks made available by waiter service. Thus, an old-fashioned atmosphere can be created by a simple menu. At intermission a menu typed on a single sheet of paper can be circulated, featuring scrambled eggs, sausage, and toast with coffee, to be served at the conclusion of the last act. Two kitchen employees can prepare and clean up for over one hundred breakfasts. In this fashion the menu can be tied-in to the program and used to assist in creating the proper atmosphere.

The Main Dining Room Menus—The menus must be developed by knowing the members and understanding why they frequent the club. It is amazing but only a small percentage of the members come to the club for just their daily sustenance! There are usually subtle reasons why one food operation is more successful than another. One of the more important is "compatible atmosphere." In using the menu to create the proper atmosphere desired, goals must first be established. These goals can also be thought of as moods:

Breakfast—Usually a bright, cheery, uncomplicated atmosphere is desired. Curtains are opened, tables are at their brightest, usually with a white table-cloth or white placemats, some yellows are visible (simulating sunlight) through table decorations. The menu should assist in sustaining this mood. One sheet of glazed cardboard simply printed with a spot of color will suffice very nicely. The menu is on the table when the member is seated and is removed when the order is placed.

Lunch—Atmosphere at this meal is almost completely created by the type of service and menu. Usually the time available to the member is limited. The member therefore expects to see that the club is ready for business (this is entirely different from hurried service, which only tends to make the member nervous).

Luncheon service is usually one of three types: table, buffet, or cafeteria. For table service the "readiness mood" is created by having the menu on one single sheet, printed on colored glazed cardboard stock placed on the table. The items that are ready are so designated, items requiring preparation time (if any are used) have the time amount noted. A leisurely atmosphere must be maintained at all costs; the member may rush the club, the club may never rush the member! Menus colored in pastel shades, printed in black with double-spaces between lines or each line indented, make for fast but relaxed reading.

The menus for buffet or cafeteria-style are best presented in two sections. The entrees are posted with prices at the entrance to the line or at table. An easel-type of stand with a colored-felt board, with white letters may be used. This gives the member the leisure necessary to select the entree in accordance with taste and pocketbook. The balance of the menu items may be printed at the serving source or on a board behind the serving line.

Dinner—The menu should be part of the total atmosphere of the dining room being created by the appearance—the decor, the lighting, and the table setting. Turn-over of place settings in a club is usually no problem. In unusual circumstances, perhaps on Mother's Day or Easter, certain clubs must use each place more than once but as this is handled by timed reservations it does not deter the basic concept of promoting leisurely, gracious dining.

In promoting such atmosphere a menu cover is usually used for dinner. This is a separate sheet of heavily glazed cardboard stock. The texture should be smooth and glossy so that it will stay crisp and clean-looking longer. Covers should be discarded as they become worn, soiled, or dog-eared.

The menu can be printed so that it encourages leisurely reading. All items are described as needed. When it is necessary to use French or other foreign names for items, a description of their meaning is included.

Other considerations must be whether or not to print the entire menu on the cover or to have a separate cover and menu.

The separate cover and menu is highly recommended as it gives management the flexibility that is needed to change the menu with the wishes of members, market availability of items, use of leftovers, season of year, outside temperature, and the speed of service. A combination of the two (printed and inserted) is becoming increasingly popular. The cover can be imprinted with the name of the club and be decorated if desired. Inside, the left side may contain a story or history or some area background information. The right side of the cover can contain four diagonal slits to hold the menu, which is separate from the cover.

However, one club, in creating a candlelight dinner, found that the proper atmosphere could only be created if all lighting was done by table candles. Obviously a regular dinner menu could not be read by most patrons so the dinner entree choice was limited to two, steak or lobster, and was announced by the waiter. The club then found that a wine was needed so a bottle of champagne was added. Now the club features a "Champagne Candlelight Dinner" for two with a choice of one of the two entrees and a bottle of champagne, which is very popular.

Other clubs have found that when soft lighting is used, such as with table candles, a menu can be read. A good menu will suggest wines from the wine list by a cross reference number. Patrons unfamiliar with their foreign names will not embarass themselves when ordering. Once more the menu-planner is creating atmosphere.

Proper menu planning can more efficiently direct the effort of the restaurant employees. The planner must always consider the fact that the items served will usually be prepared by other persons. This means that in planning these are musts:

1. Coordinate the kitchen work.
2. Have a good quantity recipe.
3. Know the finished product.
4. Have proper preparation equipment.
5. Have proper serving chinaware, glassware, and silverware.

If the planner organizes the menus in a complete working

cycle, keeping these principles in mind, control can be established for labor, providing the maximum use of all equipment.

1. Corodinate the kitchen work. Each day's menus for the meals to be prepared must be planned so that the individual meals are a part of a complete working cycle. To do this, each menu item is broken down into two time units: preparation time and cooking time. Units that can be combined in preparation for cooking are noted. For example the entire potatoes for the day will be prepared at one time but cooked at the appropriate meal hours. Other items can be grilled, baked, or roasted at one time.

   Now a closer look can be given to items that require a disproportionate amount of either preparation or cooking time and their menu strength can be evaluated. The imaginative planner discovers substitutes, keeping always in mind a minimum staff number and their capabilities. Never plan a menu to keep an overstaffed operation busy; but staff by planned unit menus.

2. Have a good quantity recipe. Good quantity recipes are not rare but some research must be done to insure the planner that the ingredients are easy to use and the cost is the lowest possible. For example, this writer, in researching a quantity recipe for a spaghetti meat sauce, found twenty-eight acceptable ways to prepare the sauce. But the cost ranged from 7 cents to 31 cents per portion and a sauce estimated at 9 cents was the easiest to prepare and was as tasty as the higher-priced item.

   The club needs a library containing some good cook books with quantity recipes.

3. Know the finished product. The planner must know what the finished product looks like when presented to the member so that the plate can be properly garnished. This knowledge must be conveyed to the kitchen staff. New items can be prepared by providing a picture of their presentation. These are easy to obtain from magazines, handouts of manufacturers, or your own photography. It should be in color. Commercial restaurants are also using these pictures as part of their menu presentation.

4. Have the proper preparation equipment. The planner knows the scope and capacity of the equipment that will be used to prepare the menus.

   The functional flexibility of the equipment limits the planner. One deep-fat fryer basket for example, could not handle fish and chicken at the same meal. Compatible items can be prepared together, a grill can handle assorted items as long as grease is controlled.

The capacity of the equipment determines the quantity of items that can be prepared. The recovery time of the fryer, the preheating times of the ovens, the area of the broiler are all factors.

5. Have proper serving equipment. The club must have the casseroles, platters, side-dishes, and other additions to serve the menu items properly. If seafood cocktails are offered, oyster forks are necessary. An 8-ounce, pear-shaped goblet is now acceptable for all wine service. The menu planner will match each item with the table service to insure that each item may properly be presented to the member.

The club can strive to operate with a 40 percent food cost, depending on the type of operation. In a well-planned menu all items do not generate the same percentage of profit. The steaks cannot be marked up as high as the poultry or seafood, so an entree study is used to determine how many of each of the main items will be sold. Usually, steaks are a good 50 percent of the business if they are priced competitively, and the percentage lost here is picked up on other items.However, this percentage can be changed by merchandising without alienating any members.

The menu is a silent salesman. It can be used to sell particular items if the menu has the proper format. Some of the ways to do this are:

1. Attach a picture of the item to be featured or leave the item off the regular menu and type or print the item as a clip-on feature.
2. Print the item in the center of the menu using different type or color.
3. Mark the item with a star or some other identifying mark, and call it the "Chef's Selection."
4. Have the server announce this item, making it sound as though this were something prepared especially for the member.
5. Use a table tent suggesting the item instead of the regular menu presentation.
6. Block it.

The Hors d'Oeuvres Menu

Trader Vic started it in his cocktail lounges. Now it has spread to many fine restaurants and clubs, it is the "hors d'oeuvres menu." This menu can feature some items of appetizers the kitchen already has prepared, such as seafood cocktails, and can be as elaborate or as simple as the manager desires. However, in every good club the manager should make some provision to serve food items in the bar. These items are served by the cocktail personnel, using duplicate guest checks and are controlled by the food checker. This is very profitable since it usually requires no additional personnel and seems only a better utilization of the server's time.

In a large club the menu may be expanded. These items have been found to be very popular:

- sesame-seed sliced pork tenderloin
- fried butterfly shrimp and fish sticks
- barbequed spareribs
- egg, shrimp, fish, and potato rolls
- fried potato skins
- mini-chicken legs
- finger sandwiches and other finger foods

The menu format is the same as that used for breakfast.

Dessert Menu

A separate dessert menu presented at the end of a meal is a very profitable idea. The server clears the table and presents the menu, ready to take orders. Here are some advantages:

1. It keeps the customer from having to give a "yes" or "no" answer to the server's "Would anyone like dessert?"
2. It spotlights desserts as an important part of a complete meal.
3. It allows space to merchandise with pictures and prose.
4. It allows for house specialties.
5. It creates a more elegant atmosphere.

Private-Party Menus

This is an old idea that has been revived successfully and that is a printed menu for the private party. It is intended as a souvenir of the party and, if done at all, must be very attractive. They can be any size, but a 3 X 5-inch format will fit into a gentleman's coat pocket or a ladies' evening bag and are more likely to be taken home than a larger one. This would be from 6 X 5-inch stock folded once. The member's name, significance of the party, date, time, and club name should appear on the front. The inside cover is used for any text (reasons and details of the occasion) with the right-hand side for the menu (without prices).

This provides a followup to the party brochure and is a very cost-effective advertising piece.

Children's Menu

A children's separate menu is always popular in a club and should feature miniatures of regular dinners along with items popular with children, such as hamburgers and hot dogs. The cut-off age should be twelve. When the child reaches his or her twelfth birthday the menu is no longer presented. Ages are not asked, the hostess or maitre d' determines from appearance alone whether to seek permission to present a child's menu to the child or to the member.

Many club managers have taken the dinner business away from the fast-food chains by selling the children's menu at food cost only. This is easy to control with guest checks and a food checker. One of the reasons parents take their families to the drive-in restaurants is not because of their own food preferences but because it is not as upsetting to see a youngster refuse a 49-cent hamburger than to watch the same child refuse a $5.00 dinner.

Many of the paper speciality companies make children's menu stock. These usually feature faces of animals and clowns on one side and a blank on the other. The faces can be worn by the child as a mask after dinner.

Menu Availability

It was the custom in "Mom-and-Pop" restaurants that, as soon as the customer made the menu selection, the menu should be removed immediately—before the customers could change their minds. Many fine restaurants and clubs still do this probably without knowing the origin, losing an opportunity to secure repeat business. Many members, after deciding what they will have, want to scan some of the other offerings for future choices. In a well-managed club the guest has a choice of handing the menu back to the server of keeping it after the order is ready. Or if the menus are so large and cumbersome they get in the way of cocktail or wine service, then they are collected by the hostess, maitre d', or waiter.

The menu is a very expensive advertising piece. It is of no use on a shelf at the dining-room reception desk. Make menus available:

- At the bar; many members who have not made dinner plans can be sold, in a very soft fashion, by their being able to see a menu without making the total commitment to entering the dining room.
- At the front reception desk and/or at the engrance to the club.
- To members to take home if they ask for them.

WINE LISTS

The pros and cons of having the wines listed on the dinner menu or on a separate wine list are many and varied. One of the reasons for a separate wine list is that since the dinner menu can be "snatched" it is better to leave a wine list. Some of the other reasons for a separate list are:

1. On a wine list the wine can be merchandised with a description. This would take up too much space on a regular menu.
2. The wine list, being smaller, can stay on the table for the entire dinner. Thus, if after the first or second course, wine is desired, the information is at hand.
3. A sommelier can be employed, to present wine lists and the wines.

The fine club will have both wines on the menu and a wine list.

Wines on the Menu

The menu will contain house wines by the carafe and popular wines, both domestic and imported wines, by the glass and bottle. This can be done by dividing the entrees into beef, other meats, seafood, and poultry (the old nomenclature of meat, fish, and fowl does not encompass enough). At the end of each grouping the manager suggests a house wine and two bottle wines. There are hundreds of wines to choose from so choose a good-to-better house wine from one of the major vineyards and from one of these three categories for the bottle wine: California, New York, or imported. In the meat groupings suggest a good white wine, either foreign or domestic.

Wine List

This provides the server with a sales tool. He can talk about wines if the member does not order wine from the food menu. This list can be beautifully presented in many fashions. Some fine clubs have a bound book with a description of each wine; others are less ostentatious but should be nice displays. The wine list is limited by the following:

- adequate storage space that is of the proper temperature
- member's tastes and interest in a fine wine cellar
- amount of money the club can invest in inventory

PROMOTING CLUB ACTIVITIES

The manager works with his staff and the various committees to promote good will and business for the club. Unlike a restaurant or hotel, which loses a customer and suffers an "iffy" loss of repeat business, if a club loses a member, it loses dues, perhaps all or part of the initiation fee, and all future business. Good will is promoted by many things but primarily by attitude. This is best expressed in club business by caring. If the manager and the employees care whether or not the member is comfortable then the club need never worry about good will. Mistakes will happen, but they will occur much less frequently if someone in charge cares.

In promoting business the manager uses every asset and all of the training and experience available. Every promotional step must be carefully worked out with the appropriate committee in coordinating a plan of action. There is such a fine line between promotion and advertising here that management must clearly understand that promoting the club is contributing to its growth and property. This is the long-range program; advertising is the short range.

For example, the promotion of the sale of wine in the dining room includes the:

- purchasing of the wine
- its proper storage
- training the employees to know the wine, know how to sell it, and know how to serve it

Advertising the wine could be effected by a display in the dining room, wine lists, and on the food menu. A poster and an article in the bulletin could also be used.

PROMOTING THE DINING ROOM

The best promotions for the dining room occur in the room itself—the courtesy and care of the dining room employees, the atmosphere of the room, and its accoutrements. However, a club dining room should have items available that not every restaurant has, such as inventive or foreign desserts, unusual coffees, etc.

PROMOTING GOURMET DINING

Gourmet dining can be promoted in many different ways. Two ways are usually sufficient for the club. One might be looked on as a gourmet club within the club membership. In this case a minimum of six persons is needed to serve a gourmet dinner to keep the price from becoming completely prohibitive. Twelve persons is the ideal with eighteen being the maximum after the club staff have had at least one year's experience. If management can arouse the interest of any one member in forming a group to dine once a month, this gives the club guaranteed patronage. One fine New England club has its own gourmet club called the "East India Company" composed of club members who dine elegantly once each three months. Another way to promote high dining is to establish a "gourmet corner" in the dining room. On request and by noncancellable advance reservation only, the club will serve a gourmet dinner to six, twelve, or eighteen persons.

THE EQUIPMENT

The list of equipment needed for gourmet dining is divided into sections. First, there are the items needed for the French service and second, the items to be set at tables.

French Service

1 gueridon (rolling cart)
2 rechauds (food warmers)
2 12-inch Flambee pans
4 8–5/8-inch casseroles with 2-inch sides
2 sets silver serving spoons and forks
4 18-inch silver serving platters

Table Linen

1 doz. white on white damask table-cloths, 54 × 108 inches
2 doz. matching serviettes, 22 × 22 inches

Silverware

24 teaspoons
24 dessert spoons
24 bouillon spoons
24 demitasse spoons
24 dinner forks

24 cocktail forks
24 salad forks
24 dinner knives
24 butter spreaders

Chinaware

24 lay plates (to be used as underliners when serving as well as
    for dinner plates)
54 bread and butter plates (can be used for salads and desserts)
18 bouillon plates
18 coffee cups
18 saucers
 2 sugar bowls with covers
 2 creamers

Glassware

15 10½ oz. Burgundy glasses
15 8½ oz. Sauterne glasses
15 5 oz. Port glasses
 2 flower vases

Miscellaneous

 2 3-pronged silver candelabra
36 glass finger bowls
18 individual salt and pepper shaker sets

THE MENU

The menus offered as part of gourmet dining can be planned by
the managers or members. However, it is recommended that if the
staff is new to this, the manager should select the complete
menu. In this fashion, training can be detailed. Later the menu
can be expanded.

The following should be some requirements of the menu:

1. Some of the items must be different than those ordinarily associated with the dining room.

2. Some of the items must lend themselves to be served with a flair and at the proper temperature when placed before the member.
3. The menu must be complete enough so that the member feels that, regardless of the price charged, he received full value for his money.
4. The items must be almost foolproof in their preparation and serving.
5. The preparation of most of the items must be a one-man job so that the kitchen is not disrupted to a point where regular service suffers.

Using these five requirements, a complete menu is selected that might suit the staff. The books used were

(1) *Chez Maxims*-McGraw Hill
(2) *The Gourmet Host*-Exposition Press
(3) *La Cuisine de France*-Orion Press

There are, however, other fine sources.

SAMPLE MENU AND RECIPES

Potage Germiny (Cream of Sorrel Soup)
Coquilles Saint-Jacques a la Parisienne (Creamed Scallops)
Poulet Saute Au Curry (Curried Chicken)
Tournedos Henri IV (Steak in Bearnaise Sauce)
Asperges a la Creme (Asparagus in Cream)
Salade Au Lard (Bacon Salad)
Sables Au Fromage (Cheese Biscuits)
Crepes Suzette (Pancakes in Cognac)
Demitasse (coffee)
Mints

Potage Germiny

Yield: 6 servings

INGREDIENTS

Bouillon Blanc (recipe follows)	1 qt.
Sorrel, fresh leaves	20 leaves
Egg Yolks	6
Butter	½ cup
Cream, heavy whipping	1 cup
Chervil, chopped	1 tsp.
Salt, pepper	

PREPARATION

Cut the sorrel leaves into narrow strips and soften them with a walnut-sized piece of butter in a deep saucepan. Pour in the Bouillon Blanc, prepared in advance (recipe follows); bring to a boil, and cook for 10 minutes. Meanwhile, beat together the cream and egg yolks. Remove the saucepan from the fire and slowly add the egg and cream mixture to the soup. Season with salt and pepper. Return saucepan to a low flame, stirring continually until a smooth, creamy consistency is obtained. Do not boil. Remove the saucepan from the fire; add the rest of the butter and chervil. Stir well and serve at once in bouillon plates.

Preparation Time: 15 minutes
Cooking Time: 10 minutes

Bouillon Blanc

This consomme is the ideal basis for many soups and sauces.

INGREDIENTS

Beef, lean	4½ lbs.
Carrots	½ lb.
Turnips	½ lb.
Parsnips	¼ cup
Leeks	½ lb.
Onions	2 medium
Garlic	2 cloves
Celery	1 stalk
Bouquet Garni*	1

PREPARATION

Quarter the carrots, turnips, parsnips, and onions; slice the leeks. Place the meat in 4 quarts of cold water and bring slowly to a boil. Skim off all the scum and fat as it comes to the surface of the liquid. Add the other ingredients and simmer for two hours, skimming at frequent intervals. Strain and continue to simmer for another 30 minutes. Pour through cheese-cloth to catch the fat.

Preparation Time: 20 minutes
Cooking Time: 3 hours

*Bouquet Garni: 1 sprig parsley, 1 sprig thyme, and 1 bay leaf, tied together.

Coquilles Saint-Jacques a la Parisienne

Yield: 6 servings

INGREDIENTS

Scallops	12
Wine, white	1 cup
Onion	1 medium
Shallot	1
Butter	6 tbsp.
Flour	3 tbsp.
Mushrooms	4 oz.
Milk	3 tbsp.
Swiss Cheese, grated	4 tbsp.
Boquet Garni*	1
Bread Crumbs	
Salt, Pepper	

PREPARATION

Cook the wine, chopped onion, shallot, bouquet garni, salt and pepper for 10 minutes. Add the scallops and cook 10 minutes longer. Meanwhile, saute the mushrooms, add and melt the rest of the butter, stir in the flour, and cook without browning for 5 minutes. Strain the cooking liquid from the scallops into flour-butter mixture; add the milk and simmer, stirring constantly, for 5 minutes. Cut 6 of the scallops and all of the mushrooms into small pieces; add these plus the 6 whole scallops to the sauce and season with salt and pepper. Simmer for 5 minutes, stirring continually. Stir in 3 tablespoons of cheese. Ladle the mixture into pyrex or scallop shells, allowing one whole scallop for each serving. Sprinkle with bread crumbs and cheese and broil until golden. Serve immediately.

Preparation Time: 30 minutes
Cooking Time: 35 minutes

*Bouquet Garni: 1 sprig parsley, 1 sprig thyme, and 1 bay leaf, tied together.

Poulet Saute Au Curry (Curried Chicken)

Yield: 6 servings

INGREDIENTS

Chicken, whole fryer	1 (3½ lb.)
Onions, medium	2
Oil (cooking)	3 tbsp.
Curry Powder	1 tbsp.
Coconut Milk	1 cup (juice from 1 coconut)
Sauce Bechamel (recipe follows)	1½ cup
Salt, Pepper	

PREPARATION

Cut up the chicken into twelve pieces and saute it in the oil until it is a golden brown color. Season with salt and pepper, add the chopped onions and curry powder, and cook slowly for 5 more minutes. Pour in the coconut milk; add the Sauce Bechamel (see recipe below). Finish cooking the chicken. Send into dining room in a heated casserole to the serving table at which the dinner plates are prepared: 2 pieces chicken on each plate with Riz a l'Indienne (steamed rice with butter), which is also sent into the dining room in a casserole.

Preparation Time: 20 minutes
Cooking Time: 45 minutes

After serving, take the casserole dishes back to the kitchen as they will be needed for service of the potatoes and the vegetable.

Sauce Bechamel (White Sauce)

Yield: 1½ cups

INGREDIENTS

Butter	2 tbsp.
Flour	2 tbsp.
Milk, scalded	1½ cups
Salt, pepper	

PREPARATION

Stir the butter and flour over a medium flame until it starts to color. Add the milk slowly, stirring constantly with a wooden spatula. The sauce should gradually thicken. Simmer for 20 minutes. Finally, season with salt.

Preparation Time: 3 minutes
Cooking time: 30 minutes

Only half of this recipe is needed for the Poulet Saute.

Tournedos Henri IV (Steak in Bearnaise Sauce)

Yield: 6 servings

INGREDIENTS

Steaks, tenderloin (prime—6 oz each)	6
Butter	3 tbsp.
Round Toast	6 slices
Salt, pepper	
Sauce Bearnaise (recipe follows)	

PREPARATION

Heat the butter in a frying pan until sizzling hot. Saute the steaks 3 to 4 minutes on each side. Season with salt and pepper. Arrange the croutons on a heated platter and place a steak on each one. Add the tarragon and remaining parsley to the Sauce Bearnaise and pour over steaks. Serve immediately with french fried potatoes.

Preparation Time: 20 minutes
Cooking Time: 6 to 8 minutes.

The platter is taken to the serving cart where the plates are prepared.

Sauce Bearnaise

Yield: 1½ cups

INGREDIENTS

Wine Vinegar	5 tbsp.
Shallots	2
Egg Yolks	5
Butter	6 tbsp.
Parsley, chopped	3 tsp.
Tarragon, chopped	1 tsp.
Salt	
Pepper, freshly ground	

PREPARATION

Prepare the Sauce Bearnaise first. Simmer the vinegar, 3 tbsp. of water, the chopped shallots, ½ of the parsley, and a good dash of pepper for 5 minutes. Melt the butter in the top of a double boiler, stir in the egg yolks, and continue stirring over hot, but not boiling, water until the mixture thickens. Slowly strain in the hot vinegar, beating constantly. Season with salt. Keep hot.

Asperges a la Creme (Asparagus with Cream Sauce)

Yield: 6 servings

INGREDIENTS

Asparagus	4 lbs.
Sauce Bechamel	1½ cups
Cream, heavy	½ cup
Lemon	½
Salt	

PREPARATION

Peel the asparagus stalks carefully. Wash in cold water, drain, and cook in gently boiling salted water. When the asparagus is tender but still firm, drain and place in warm water until ready to serve. Reduce the Sauce Bechamel by half. Heat the cream and add it to the sauce.

Stir until you have the consistency of sour cream. Season with salt and the juice of ½ lemon. Drain the asparagus stalks and place on a serviette in a warmed casserole. Serve the cream sauce in a gravy boat.

Preparation Time: 25 minutes
Cooking Time: 10 minutes

The asparagus and the sauce will go to the cart and be served on a separate plate along with an entree and potatoes.

Salade Au Lard (Bacon Salad)

Yield: 6 servings

INGREDIENTS

Watercress, young	½ lb.
Chicory or Romaine	½ lb.
Bacon	4 oz.
Vinegar, white	2 tbsp.
Salt, pepper	

PREPARATION

Pick over, wash, and dry the salad greens. Put them in a deep, ceramic salad bowl and place in a slightly preheated oven. Dice and fry the bacon; when it is done, pour it and the hot fat over the greens. Pour the vinegar quickly into the same pan; stir, heating slightly, and pour over the salad. Season with pepper and a little salt. Toss and serve.

Preparation Time: 15 minutes
Cooking Time: 10 minutes

Sables Au Fromage (Cheese Biscuits)

Yield: 20 biscuits

INGREDIENTS

Butter, soft, sweet	9 tbsp.
Pastry Flour, sifted	1½ cups + 1 tbsp.
Gruyere Cheese	1¼ cups
Salt	¼ tsp.

PREPARATION

Mix all the ingredients together by hand until the dough is well blended. Preheat the oven to 400° (204°C). Roll out the dough on a floured surface to a thickness of ¼ inch. With a glass or cookie cutter, cut out rounds and place them on a lightly buttered baking sheet. Bake 10 minutes or until browned lightly at the edges. Watch carefully as these bisquits cook very quickly, and the time needed depends entirely on the thickness of the pastry.

Preparation Time: 10 minutes
Cooking Time: Approx. 10 minutes

Some of these will be sent into the dining room on a serviette placed in a bread basket. A small plate with a butter cube will be put down at this time in front of each guest when the biscuits are presented. If the diner indicates that he or she wants them, the server, using tongs or serving spoon and fork, transfers two from the basket to the plate. The basket is then returned to the kitchen to go into a warmer. The server watches to see when the biscuits are eaten so that they may be passed again as desired.

Crepes Suzette (Pancakes in Cognac)

Yield: 6 servings

INGREDIENTS

Flour, sifted	2 cups
Eggs	4
Sugar	½ cup
Milk	2 cups
Butter, melted	¼ cup
Vanilla	
Salt	

PREPARATION

Mix the flour, sugar, and a pinch of salt together in a bowl. Stir in the eggs, one at a time, a drop of vanilla, and the warmed milk, stirring constantly with a wooden spatula. The batter should be smooth and just thick enough to coat the spatula. If too thick, add more milk. Finally, add the melted butter and stir until homogeneous. Cover and chill for at least an hour before use. Cook the crepes in a large, moderately heated, buttered pan, putting in just enough batter to cover the bottom. Brown lightly, shake to loosen, turn and brown the other side very lightly. Keep warm until needed in a moderate oven 350°F. (177°C) Regrease the pan between each crepe.

Preparation Time: 10 minutes
Cooking Time: 10 minutes

The crepes will be sent into the dining room on a heated platter. Do not stack
the crepes, but interleaf them.

The last items of the menu are the Demitasse (coffee) and
mints. The coffee is served in cups placed on the table after the
Crepe plates have been removed. The mints are placed on the
table at the same time.

THE WINES

The menu will be complemented with the serving of four wines
with the dinner. A serving is four ounces, six servings from each
bottle. Compute the price accordingly. In planning the party,
explain to the host the price includes one four-ounce serving of
each wine, but that he may purchase as many bottles as he
desires.

In preparing the items of glassware that are recommended,
it is anticipated that champagne saucers or hollow-stem goblets
will be used.

The pleasing harmony that can be achieved by matching the
wine and food flavors can turn even the most ordinary meal
into an event. With this elegant menu, carefully select the wines.

Start serving the first wine between the soup and the seafood course. This must be a very subtle, very light wine. Some
Alsace-type Rieslings or Chablis would be suitable. Use the port
glass.

With curried chicken it is recommended that a very light
red wine be served. Some Bordeaux wines would harmonize
very well. Use the Sauterne glass.

With the steak, a full-bodied red wine, such as a Burgundy,
would cleanse the taste buds. Use the Burgundy glass.

With the crepes, serve champagne. Use a champagne that is
just a little bit sweet (it will have "SEC" on the label). It should
harmonize beautifully, finishing the meal.

THE TRAINING

One of the types of service that the manager will offer in gourmet dining could be "French service." In Europe and England high-class table service has followed a somewhat similar pattern for several generations. This pattern involves the use of silver serving pieces, the heating and garnishing of food at a side table (or gueridon), and the serving of portions to the guests on heated plates either by a server, an assistant, or sometimes by the host. In its most elaborate form, this service may be called "Service a la Ritz" after Cesar Ritz who founded a line of luxury hotels early in the twentieth century. In America, this service is commonly known as "French service," and its use is declining because it requires professional waiters. Before World War II most professional waiters in America received their training in Europe. This training involved several years' apprenticeship, coupled with regular classes at a professional waiter's school, leading toward becoming a *commis de rang* comparable to the regular American waiter. In Europe, however, a *commis de rang* is not considered a "perfect waiter" and cannot work alone. He works with a *demi-chef de rang* or a *chef de rang* for another two or three years until he receives the status of "perfect waiter," or *chef de rang*. However, with a training plan and some all-out effort on the manager's part, the staff can be trained. Many managers have done this already and have now, or have had, French service in their dining rooms.

In French service, two waiters usually tend one station. One is called *chef de rang* and the other, *commis de rang*. These two work as a team. Each has specific duties but helps the other when needed. The duties of the chef de rang follow:

- Seat the guests if there is no head waiter
- Take the orders of the guest
- Serve all drinks
- Finish the preparation of the food at the table in front of the guests
- Present the check

The main duties of the *commis* follow:

- Receive the orders from the *chef de rang,* take them to the kitchen and order the food
- Pick up the food in the kitchen and bring the food on a tray into the dining room and over to the rolling cart
- Serve the plate of food to the guest which the *chef de rang* has prepared
- Help the *chef de rang* whenever he can

Setting the Table

Place a plate at the cover just a fraction of an inch from the table's edge, with a neatly folded serviette on the plate. The dinner fork goes to the left of the plate (close to the table's edge) and the dinner knife to the right of the plate with the cutting edge toward the plate. The soup spoon is placed beside and to the right of the dinner knife, the butter plate and the butter knife (laid across the plate parallel to the dinner fork) to the left of the dinner fork. The dessert fork and spoon go above the plate as these pieces are not used until the dessert is served. Then the glasses are placed above the tip of the dinner knife.

In French service the glasses are not placed upside-down on the table prior to filling them, because it gives European guests the impression that the dining room is not ready to serve. When tables are set up an hour or two ahead of serving time, the glasses may be turned upside-down at the cover to prevent dust falling into them; but before the dining room is ready to open the server goes around the station turning them right-side up.

Since coffee is not served during dinner, coffee spoons are placed on the table only when needed. Coffee, if served, comes after the dessert. The coffee spoon is placed to the right of the cup and on top of the underliner, when the demitasse is put down.

The Service

French service differs from other services in that all food is served from a gueridon (cart). The gueridon, covered with a tablecloth, is kept close to the guest's table. It must have a rechaud to keep food warm. The gueridon should be the same height as the guest's table.

In French service, the food is partially prepared by the chef in the kitchen, and is "finished" by the *chef de rang* in view of the guests. Food is brought into the dining room on an attractive silver platter by the *commis de rang* who sets it on the rechaud to keep warm. The *chef de rang* then takes over, carving the meat, boning the chicken, and making the sauce or any garnishes required.

The *commis de rang* holds the guest plate below the silver platter while the *chef de rang,* using both hands, transfers food to the guest's plate. The *chef de rang* may hold the serving fork and spoon in one hand, to leave one hand free. This practice is acceptable when no *commis* is near to help, so that the plate must be held while serving the food.

As the *chef de rang* serves the food, the eyes are kept on the guest to see how much the guest wants. Filling the plate too full diminishes the appetite and enjoyment of the gourmand.

Once the food has been arranged on the plate, the *commis de rang* takes the plate in the right hand and serves it to the guest's right side.

In French service, everything is served from the right with the exception of the butter and the bread plates, salad plates, and any other extra dish which should be placed at the left side of the guest. Every rule has its reason. To serve food from the right is much easier for a right-handed server as the plate can be carried in the right hand, and the tray set in front of the guest from the right. It is difficult and awkward to serve a plate with the right hand from the left side. The exception to the rule is when a server is left-handed, then service is from the left instead of the right.

Soup

The soup course is brought into the dining room in a silver bowl and placed on the rechaud to keep warm. More soup than needed is always brought in. Soup not ladled out into the guest's soup plate is brought back to the chef and reheated to serve other guests (if allowed by state law).

The *commis* also brings hot soup plates. The soup plate is then placed on a plate with a square folded serviette in between the plate and the soup plate. This serves a dual purpose: 1) it makes it possible for the waiter to carry the plate without getting burned; and 2) it prevents the waiter from putting his thumb into the soup. This service is more attractive than placing only the regular soup plate before the guest. The soup is ladled from the silver bowl into the soup plate by the *chef de rang* and served to the guest by the *commis* from the right with the right hand.

Main Course

The main course, or any other course in French service, is served in the same manner as the soup course. The *chef de rang* always does the carving, preparing, or flaming of a course, and arranges it on the guest's plate; the *commis* serves it. Salad is served with the main course and placed below the butter plate with the left hand from the left side of the guest.

The Correct Way to Hold Plates

Plates should be held with the thumb, index finger, and the middle finger. The upper part of the plate's rim should not be touched; this prevents fingers from getting into the soup or leaving marks on the plate. The technique is not so difficult as it sounds, but it does require regular practice.

Clearing the Table

All soiled dishes are removed from the table after each course is consumed and before a new course is served. The slowest eater sets the pace and no plates are ever removed until everyone has completed the course. This gives the guest an opportunity to dine leisurely and to enjoy the service and the food. After the main course is removed make sure the waiter is trained to brush the cloth to remove bread crumbs. Any stains that occur on the cloth during the meal are covered immediately with a clean serviette.

Remove all the plates from each course in one round of the

table, when possible. Do not scrape or stack plates in front of the guests; remember this is gourmet dining. Clearing a table requires training and practice if it is to be done smoothly. Make sure that the salt and pepper shakers are removed with the main course dishes as the stage is being set for the *piece de resistance,* the dessert.

Finger Bowl

Finger bowls are served with all dishes that the guest eats with his fingers; such as chicken, lobster, and fresh fruit. The finger bowl is a small silver or glass bowl placed on the underliner plate with a doily in between the bowl and the underliner. A clean, extra serviette is served with it. The finger bowl is filled only one-third full with warm water to prevent splashing. A lemon wedge or flower petals are often put into the water.

The finger bowl is served with the courses mentioned above, not afterwards. When a guest eating lobster with his fingers suddenly wishes a sip of wine, he washes his fingers before touching the glass. If possible, place the finger bowl in front of the plate. An additional finger bowl is always served at the end of any complete meal in French service and is placed directly in front of the guest with a fresh serviette.

Setups for Special Dishes

As experience is gained, expand. Here are some items to expand upon:

Cold or hot lobster and langouste—cold or hot dinner plates (depending on whether the lobster is served hot or cold), fish fork and fish knife, lobster fork, nut cracker, butter plate and butter knife, and finger bowl.

Caviar—Cold hors d'oeuvre plate, small hors d'oeuvre fork and knife, teaspoon, butter plate and butter knife.

Oysters and clams—Oysters or clams are usually served arranged on crushed ice on silver platters. Many times this silver platter is placed in front of the guest with no extra plate. On other occasions the oysters are placed in the center of the table, the guest having an hors d'oeuvre plate on which to place his oysters. An oyster fork, butter plate and butter knife, and a finger bowl are also included.

Whole grilled snails—Hot dinner plate, snail fork, snail tongs, butter plate and butter knife, and finger bowl are needed. The snails (fried in the shell and then arranged on a bed of heated salt on a silver platter) are placed in the center of the table. The snails are picked up with the snail tongs by the guest and are eaten with the special snail fork.

Fresh fruits—Fruit or dessert plate, fruit fork and fruit knife, and finger bowl are necessary for most fresh fruits. There are some exceptions, such as mangos and papayas.

Fresh grapes—Fresh grapes require a special service. The cover consists of a fruit or dessert plate, a crystal bowl or champagne saucer filled with ice water, a pair of scissors, fruit fork and fruit knife, and a finger bowl. The reason for this elaborate setup is that in French service the bunch of grapes is served in a crystal bowl in the center of the table. The guest then takes the pair of scissors, clips off a bunch of grapes, washes them in the ice water and then puts the grapes on his plate. He eats the grapes with his fingers or uses the fruit fork and knife to peel off the skin and take out the seeds.

Flaming

Flaming adds little to a dish but it presents a gala and profitable display, so encourage it. Flaming impresses the guest. The server, while flaming the dessert at one table, catches the attention of other people in the dining room and advertises gourmet dining. In flaming, the principle is always the same. The sauce or liqueur used is the only variation.

One of the world's most popular desserts is crepes suzettes. Like other famous dishes, crepes suzettes were first served quite by accident about a hundred years ago.

Henri Charpentier, chef to Edward, Prince of Wales, was making a complicated crepe sauce. This sauce was a blend of orange and lemon peels, sugar, butter, Grand Marnier, Cointreau, and Kirschwasser. By accident, the cordial caught fire and the young chef thought both he and his sauce were ruined. Since it was impossible to start again, Henri tasted the sauce and found it was delicious. He quickly put the crepes into the liquid, added more cordials, and let the sauce burn again.

The Prince was delighted with the new dessert and named it after the lady with whom he was dining.

Crepe Suzette Sauce

Yield: 6 servings

INGREDIENTS

sugar	¾ cup
orange	½
lemon	½
butter	½ cup
Cognac	1½ oz.
Grand Marnier	1½ oz.
Cointreau	1½ oz.

PREPARATION

Sprinkle granulated sugar on hot pan, wait until sugar melts. Cut some orange and then some lemon peel and put them into the pan— stir with sugar. Hold the fruit in a serviette. Add butter, wait until it melts. Squeeze orange and lemon juice into pan, removing orange and lemon peels. Put crepes into pan; unroll, warm, and turn them. Roll crepes and let them simmer in juice. Add some more granulated sugar on top of crepes. Add Grand Marnier, Cointreau, and Cognac (brandy). Dip the pan so the flame below touches the Cognac and ignites the whole sauce. Serve crepes, using fork and spoon, on hot dessert plates.

As mentioned before, French service has its grandeur, and French service gives the member the greatest possible personal attention. It makes the member feel very important—it is royal treatment and very showy. This then is what "Gourmet Dining" with French Service is all about! Now to the specifics of implementation. The areas that are critical and will require much effort are all in the dining room. With very little practice, anyone with a basic knowledge of the kitchen can produce the suggested menu above or one similar to it. This will hold true for about 75 percent of the items in the *Chez Maxims*. A must, however, is that until the top kitchen person has at least six months experience, plan to relieve him or her from all other duties on gourmet night. Many items may have to be specially purchased; some of the items can be prepared well in advance. But anticipate no problems in the kitchen. The problem is to develop a working team with the chef, the *chef de rang,* and the *commis de rang.* This can best be done by carefully selecting the personnel who are going to participate, with substitutes, and sell them on the program before you start.

Keep in mind the three objectives:

1. To enhance the image of a topnotch professional manager
2. To offer the members something new and different
3. To get the staff completely involved and interested in their business

To achieve one, management must accomplish all! Get the entire staff involved then. Make sure that everyone, whether participating actively in the gourmet dining or not, understands what is going on.

Training the Chef

The secret is timing. French service is designed to be slow to promote leisurely dining. The chef must practice to be able to prepare each dish confidently. There is a need to know the consumption time. The menu suggested would take a minimum of two hours to serve and consume. It might, if the party was having a good time, take up to three-and-a-half hours. The Chef must practice and the way to do this is to put certain selected items on the regular menu on slow nights. Some items, such as the soups, salads, vegetables, and bread items can be served unannounced as a special treat to the customers. The entrees and more expensive items could be announced by the server as a particular evening's special. Do not plan to serve more than one item in any one evening since care must be taken not to take the "bloom" from the complete menu.

Training the Commis de Rang

The *commis de rang* works directly for and is responsible to the *chef de rang.*

The most difficult part of this job is transferring items

from trays to plates that are already on the table in front of the member. In the menu selected, there is only one item that would be handled—the bisquits—but this must be done correctly, using tongs, although traditionally the server would use a tablespoon and fork. The other things to be practiced are serving plates with sauces and liquids on them, keeping them absolutely level, and clearing the table.

As part of the training, when the chef is practicing such things as making bisquits and other items, have bread and butter plates on the table and have the server present this item "French style."

If the spoon and fork are used, teach the server to handle them as if they were chopsticks—just turn the wrist so that the bowl of the spoon is held horizontal. A good practice device—a flat tray and round items, such as onions; the server transfers the onions into a bowl of water without a splash.

The server must also practice serving liquids, such as coffee, wine, etc.

Just a little practice goes a long way to give the server confidence.

Training the Chef de Rang

This is the position that holds the key to the success or failure of the "French service." This employee controls the entire dining room operation, directs the *commis de rang* as to when and what food course to bring from the kitchen, prepares the plates, and directs the *commis de rang* in serving them. Usually the *chef de rang* also indicates when the dishes are to be picked up.

Normally, the *chef de rang* will serve all drinks including the wine; but if rushed (or it seems more practical) the *commis de rang* may do this.

The *chef de rang* must practice—but not on the members. This must be done privately and the practice sessions should involve the manager. The manager can break down the various segments of the job and schedule the practices.

1. Food handling, cutting, and arranging the items on the plate; set up practice sessions the same as done for the *commis de rang*.

2. Using the rechauds; each tray coming from the kitchen should rest on the rechaud if it is to be served hot while the plate is prepared.

3. Setting up the serving table; the *chef de rang* must study the menu and have on the table those items that will be needed to furnish the food item.

4. Using the pan for flambe dishes; there are a few simple safety rules that must be taught as well as "skill with the skillet." The rechaud and the crepe pan are hot. The hotter the pan, the hotter the alcohol, the higher the flame. Starting with a hot pan, for example with crepe suzettes, the ingredients should cool it down so that the alcohol is warm enough to ignite, but not hot enough to flash.

5. Memorizing the recipes for making the various dishes; the *chef de rang* cannot use any notes, the knowledge must be there.

Wine Service

If the manager wishes, get one of the wineries to assist in the training of personnel. However, serving wine at a gourmet dinner is just a little different.

1. It is assumed that the host has selected the wines in advance. Thus, there is no elaborate ceremony in opening the bottles. Ladies are served first.

2. Each used wine glass is removed from the table as the plates for that course are removed. If there is still wine in the glass, the *commis de rang* asks whether the guest is finished with it.

PROMOTING WINE SALES IN THE DINING ROOM

Promoting the sale of wine in a club is relatively easy as regards the member but where the difficulty lies is getting the serving employees to implement the promotion program. The members are usually used to have wine with meals and management's responsibility is to

- provide a good wine selection for the member to choose from
- see that the wines are held at the proper temperature
- train the employees to serve the wine properly

The more that the manager knows about wines the easier it becomes to train the employees. To start, all wines are divided into two types, generic and varietal, and five classes. Generic wines are those named for the original place they were produced and are wines such as Burgundy, Chablis, Sauturne, Rhine, and Chianti.

Even though many American generic wines may not always resemble in flavor the European counterparts for which they were named, the quality of most brands is excellent. That is not the case with all brands, but the same applies to their European cousins—some are great and some are mediocre.

The other type of wines are the varietals.

Varietal wines, regardless of where they are grown, all carry the same name as the grapes from which they were made. Pinot Noir is made from Pinot Noir grapes, Cabernet Sauvignon wine is made from Cabernet Sauvignon grapes, Pinot Chardonnay wine is made from Pinot Chardonnay grapes, and Chenin Blanc wine is made from Chenin Blanc grapes. So, it is easy to remember the name of the varietal wine. The word "name," as is being used, refers to the name of the "type" of wine not the brand name. There are many different brand names for the same type of varietal or the same generic wine. A few of the same varietal wines with different brand names are Almaden Pinot Chardonnay and Paul Masson Pinot Chardonnay. And some of the same generic wines with different brand names are Almaden Chablis, Paul Masson Chablis and Barton and Guestier Chablis. With respect to vin rosés, there are Lancer's and Mateus from Portugal, Nectarose from the Anjou district of France, and some excellent California products.

The American government permits wineries to declare a wine a particular varietal by putting the name of the grape on the label if 51 percent or more of the wine in the bottle is made from that particular grape.

In addition to Chablis being made only in the area so designated, the Pinot Chardonnay grape is the only grape that can be used to make wine labeled "Chablis." Therefore, some Pinot Chardonnays will have characteristics of, and be similar to, the better Chablis from France. Some French Chablis are of poor quality. That is why the shipper or brand name is so important, and why such great care must be exercised in the selection of the wines for the club wine list.

The varietal wines on the wine list are Chenin Blanc, Pinot Chardonnay, Grey Riesling, Traminer, Pinot Noir, Cabernet Sauvignon, Gamay Beaujolais, Zinfandel, and Charbono.

1. Appetizer wines such as sherry and vermouth
2. Red table wines such as Burgundy and Chianti
3. White table wines such as Sauterne and Chablis
4. Dessert wines such as port and Madiera
5. Sparkling wines such as champagne and sparkling Burgundy

Appetizer Wines

Appetizer wines are so called because they are favored for before meal or cocktail use. The main appetizer wines are sherry and vermouth. They range from extra dry to sweet, the drier types more suitable for serving when too sweet a beverage may fail to sharpen appreciation of the food to follow. The new special natural wines also are used as appetizers, as well as all-purpose refreshment beverages.

Sherry—Often made from the Palomino grape, sherry is the most popular of all appetizer wines. It is characterized by its nutty flavor obtained from aging at warm temperatures. It ranges in color from pale to dark amber and is made either extra dry, dry, medium dry or sweet. The sweet type (used less as an appetizer than as a dessert or refreshment wine) sometimes is called "cream" or "golden" Sherry. The alcoholic content of Sherry is about 20 percent.

Vermouth—Vermouth is a wine flavored with herbs and other aromatic substances. There are two principal types: dry (French), sweet (Italian). The dry is pale amber, the sweet, dark amber. Along with the traditional dry vermouth, there has been developed, in recent years, a type called light dry vermouth. This has the general characteristics of dry vermouth but is extremely pale—almost colorless.

In producing Vermouth, neutral white wines first are selected and aged. Then they are flavored, either by steeping the herbs in the wine or by adding an infusion of herbs.

Vermouth ranges from 15 to 20 percent in alcoholic content.

Red Dinner Wines

Burgundy. Burgundy is a generous, full-bodied, dry red wine, traditionally heavier in flavor, body, and bouquet, and of a deeper red color than clarets. California Burgundy is made from one or more of a number of grape varieties including Gamay, Petite Sirah, Pinot Noir, and Refosco. Burgundy and Claret often are made from the same grapes. A blend producing a lighter-bodied wine is called Claret, the heavier bodied wine is called Burgundy.

Pinot-Noir, Gamay, Red Pinot. Burgundy type wines, the first two of which are named for the grapes from which they are made, with the flavors and aromas of their respective grapes of red burgundy-type wines. The California wine made from it has a velvety soft body and a deep, rich bouquet. Red Pinot type may be made from one or more of several red or black Pinot grape varieties.

Barbera and Charbono. Barbera may be said to fit within the broad Burgundy group because they are full bodied, but are far heavier-bodied and tarter than most Burgundys.

Claret. The name popularly applies to any dry, pleasantly tart, light, or medium-bodied dinner wine of ruby-red color. Wines of this type are the most widely used mealtime wines in almost every wine-drinking country in the world. California wines marketed under the broad title of Claret are made from one or more of a number of grape varieties such as Cabernet Sauvignon, Ruby Cabernet, Carignane, Mataro, Mondeuse, and Zinfandel. It is not unusual for a claret to be made from one of the grapes used for Burgundy, though the blend would be light-bodied.

Zinfandel. Zinfandel is a claret-type made from the Zinfandel grape and has its distinctive fruity taste and aroma. It is produced only in California.

Cabernet Sauvignon. Cabernet Sauvignon is a claret-type wine that has been made from and has the distinct, fruity-taste and aroma of the Cabernet Sauvignon grape. It is stronger in flavor and bouquet than most other clarets, and in California often is fuller-bodied and deeper in color than Burgundy, particularly when made from the Cabernet Sauvignon, the traditional grape variety for clarets. Cabernet can be made from several other Cabernet grapes, but it then is "Cabernet" not "Cabernet Sauvignon."

Grignolino. This claret-type wine is named for the grape from which it is made and has the distinct flavor and aroma of that grape. Grignolinos have a decided orange-red color and are made more like Rosés. The lighter blends sometimes are labeled "Rosé."

Rosé. A pink dinner wine sometimes called a luncheon wine. It has also been called the "all-purpose wine" because of its versatility. Rosé wines range from dry to slightly sweet, are usually fruity-flavored, light-bodied and made from the Cabernet, Gamay, Grenache and Grignolino grapes.

Vine Rosso (or Mellow Red). This generalized term is applied to a type of red dinner wine that, like Rosé, has climbed rapidly in popularity in recent years. "Rosso" wines, also known as "mello red wines," often are labeled with Italian-type names indicating they are "family wines." They usually are slightly sweet to semisweet, medium to heavy-bodied, ruby-red in color, blander and softer in flavor than traditional red dinner wines. Their alcoholic content is the same as that of other red dinner wines (10–14 percent).

Other Dinner Wines

Red Chianti. In color and body the red dinner wine known as Chianti may resemble either Claret or Burgundy. Chianti usually is dry, fruity, slightly tart, ruby red. Traditionally it is made from Sangioveto grapes, but other grapes often are used.

Concord, Ives, Norton. Red dinner wines with the characteristic flavors, aromas and tartness of the corresponding grapes that are grown in the Eastern United States. Concord ranges from semisweet to very sweet and is classed a dessert wine. The Ives and Norton usually make a dryer wine.

White Dinner Wines

White dinner wines vary from extremely dry and tart to sweet and full-bodied, with the delicate flavor that blends

best with white meat, fowl, and seafood. They range from pale
straw to deep gold in color, and in alcoholic content from
10 to 14 percent. The most popular white dinner wines are
Chablis, Rhine wine, and Sauterne, and most other white dinner
wines resemble these three broad types.

Chablis. Chablis is a white dinner wine that is very dry with
a fruity flavor and a delicate gold color. It is slightly fuller-
bodied and less tart than Rhine wine. Traditionally it is made
from a number of white Burgundy grape varieties, notably the
aristocratic Pinot Blanc and the Chardonnay. True-to-type
Chablis wines are made in this country from these grapes, and
also from Burger, Golden Chasselas, Green Hungarian, and
several other varieties.

Chardonnay, Pinot Blanc, Folle Blanche, Chenin Blanc.
Chablis type wines, named for their grapes and having their
distinct flavors and aromas. Chardonnay sometimes is referred
to as Pinot Chardonnay. Chenin Blanc is made from the Chenin
Blanc grape. This grape also produces wines labeled as White
Pinot, which vary from dry to quite sweet.

Rhine Wine. Rhine wine is the generic name popularly
applied to any thoroughly dry, pleasantly tart, light-bodied
white dinner wine, pale golden or slightly green-gold. The
original Rhine wines were made from only a few special grapes,
notably the Riesling varieties, but wines of many other grapes
are classed as Rhine wines in this country, as well. Often they
are bottled in an extra tall, tapered bottle.

Riesling. Riesling is a Rhine wine made from one of the
Riesling variety grapes and having its particular flavor and
aroma. The best known California Riesling is produced from the
true Johannisberg Riesling grape (also called White Riesling).
There also are Grey Riesling and Franken Riesling (Sylvaner)
wines made from the corresponding grapes.

Traminer, Sylvaner. Rhine wines named for the grapes
from which they are made, and having their distinct flavors and
aromas. Sylvaner is known also as Franken Riesling.

Hock and Moselle. Other names for Rhine type wines.
They have separate geographic significance in European wines,
but none in the United States. The name hock is used in English-
speaking countries as a synonym for Rhine wine.

Sauterne. Sauternes are golden-hued, fragrant, full-bodied, white dinner wines ranging from dry to sweet. There are three kinds of Sauternes in the United States—Dry Sauterne, Sauterne, and Sweet, Haut or Chateau Sauterne. The wide variations are explained by the fact that the sweetness of the three Sauterne types is not defined by regulation. California Sauternes, however, are generally drier than those of France. Traditionally, Sauterne is a blend of three grape varieties—Semillon, Sauvignon Blanc, and Muscadelle du Bordelais—but a wide assortment of other white grape varieties also is used in the United States.

Savignon Blanc, Samillon. Sauterne type wines named for the grapes from which they are made, with the flavors and aromas of their respective grape varieties. Both are usually dry, but sometimes are made either semi-sweet or sweet.

Other White Dinner Wines

White Chianti. While it sometimes resembles either Rhine or Chablis, White Chianti is usually typically Italian and quite robust for a white. It is dry, somewhat fruity, slightly tart, medium-bodied. Customarily it is made from a combination of Trebbiano and a Muscat-flavored grape.

Light Muscat. Dinner wines made from Muscat grapes, with the characteristic Muscat flavor and aroma, have gained in popularity in recent years. They usually are called Light Muscat wine but sometimes simply Sweet White Wine. While always unmistakable because of the Muscat character, Light Muscats vary from completely dry to very sweet. When made from special Muscat grape varieties, Light Muscat sometimes is labeled with the exact variety name, such as Muscat Canelli or Muscat Frontignan.

Catawba, Delaware, Elvira, Scuppernong. White dinner wines, grown in the East and Midwest of the United States, with the typical flavors, aromas and tartness of the grapes for which they are named. Catawba is produced both dry and semi-sweet, like Sauterne, while Delaware and Elvira have more Rhine wine characteristics. Scuppernong is light amber and usually is a sweet light Sauterne. Delaware is closer to a Rhine wine.

Dessert Wines

Sweet, full-bodied wines served with desserts, or as refreshments, are called dessert wines. Their alcoholic content is usually about 20 percent. They range from medium-sweet to sweet and from pale gold to red.

The three distinct popular types are Port, Muscatel and Tokay.

Port. Port is a rich, fruity, heavy-bodied, sweet wine, usually deep red. There is a lighter-bodied Port, called Tawny Port, usually made from grapes less rich in color than used for Red Port. There also is White Port that is strawcolored. Originating in Portugal, also the birthplace of Red Port, it is said to have been produced first for sacramental use.

Ports may be made from one or more of a dozen grape varieties including Carignane, Petite Sirah, Tinta Cao, Tinta Madeira, Trousseau and Zinfandel.

Muscatel. Muscatel is a rich, flavorful, sweet dessert wine made from Muscat grapes and having their unmistakable flavor and aroma. Its color ranges from golden or dark amber to red. While most Muscatel is made from the Muscat of Alexandria grape and is golden, at least seven other Muscat grape varieties are used in California to make Muscatels of varying flavors.

Red Muscatel, Black Muscatel. Muscatels that are red, or dark red, sometimes made from Black Muscat (Muscat Hamburg) grapes.

Muscat Frontignan, Muscat Canelli are made from a special variety of Muscat grape. Both names refer to the same grape.

Tokay. Tokay has an important place among dessert wines because its sweetness is midway between that of Sherry and Port. It is amber colored and has a slightly "nutty," or Sherry flavor. It is made by blending other dessert wines, usually Angelica, Port, and Sherry. California Tokay is not to be confused with the Tokay wine of Hungary, to which it has no similarity except in sweetness or with the Flame Tokay grape that may, or may not, be used in its production.

Other Sweet Dessert Wines

Angelica. Angelica is a white dessert wine, resembling White Port. Traditionally the sweetest of the standard wine types, it is either straw or amber colored and mild and fruity, like a cordial. Angelica originated in California and is produced from a number of grape varieties, including Grenache and Mission.

Kosher Wines. The term "Kosher" can be applied to any wine certified by a rabbi. Thus, Kosher wines can be any type, red or white, and of varying alcoholic content and sweetness. For example, there are Kosher Ports and Kosher Sherries produced in California and other states. However, the largest production is of a very sweet, red Kosher wine made largely from Concord grapes in eastern states where the addition of cane or beet sugar is permitted.

Sparkling Wines

Sparkling wines are dinner wines (enjoyed also with appetizers or desserts, or without food) that have been made naturally effervescent by a second fermentation in closed containers. They are red, pink, or white, and have a wide flavor range. Their alcoholic content usually extends from 10 to 14 percent by volume, as does that of still dinner wines. The most popular types are Champagne and Sparkling Burgundy.

Champagne. Champagne is generally pale gold or straw colored. The driest Champagne is called *nature;* that which is very dry usually is labeled *brut;* semi-dry generally is labeled *sec* or *dry,* and sweet is labeled *doux.*

Champagne is made from one or more of many grape varieties, by tradition from Chardonnay, Pinot Blanc, or Pinot Noir, the latter a black grape. It is also made from Burger, Emerald Riesling, Folle Blanche, French Colombard Green Hungarian, St. Emilion, Sauvignon Vert, and other grapes such as Catawba, Delaware and Elvira.

Pink Champagne. The Pinot Noir, or one or more of the dark skinned Champagne grapes, is used to make the wine base for Pink Champagne. The pink color results from letting the juice remain with the grape skins during fermentation until the desired hue is obtained.

Sparkling Burgundy. Sparkling Burgundy is red wine made sparkling by the same methods as is Champagne. It is usually semi-sweet or sweet. Barbera, Carignane, Mondeuse, Petite Sirah and Pinot Noir are the grapes favored for its production.

Champagne Rouge is similar to Sparkling Burgundy.

Other Sparkling Wines

Sparkling Muscat. Champagne-like wine of Muscat flavor, made from light Muscat wines, usually from Muscat Canelli grapes. Also called Moscato Spumante.

Sparkling Rosé. Similar to Pink Champagne, but usually made from the same specific grapes preferred for Rosé dinner wine.

Crackling wines. There are a few wines, less effervescent than champagne, which are known as *crackling, petillant* or *frizzante.* In this country they must be made by a natural second fermentation within the bottle, or a closed container.

Carbonated wines. Wines and red wines, both dry and sweet, occasionally are made effervescent by artifical carbonation. Because of a lower tax rate, they usually are less expensive than the natural sparkling wines.

Red wine should be served at cool room temperature and white wine should be chilled. But some people like all wine chilled so the wine will have to be served the way the members want it, and graciously. They just might even be wine experts experimenting or have individualistic tastes they like to pamper.

If the members are wine experts, they will expect the server to show them the bottle before it is opened as a courtesy that they are receiving what they asked for. Also they will expect the server not to rip all the foil off the neck of the bottle, but to cut it neatly near the top; and to wipe the cork and top of the bottle before the corkscrew is inserted. Always train the employee to screw completely through the cork before attempting to draw it, and to wipe inside the rim of the neck and top of the bottle carefully again after the cork is pulled. The host will also expect the server to sniff the bottom of the cork to determine if the wine is "corky" and then to give him the cork to test. Corky wine is one that has a definite and disagreeable flavor and will flavor the cork. It is so seldom that wine is "corky" that you will be safe in training the server to go through the motions even if he or she is not sure of the wine quality.

If it is a bottle of red wine being served in a wine basket, hold the basket so the bottle remains tilted. The server does not shake it or raise it to an upright position so that if there is sediment in the bottle it will remain undisturbed. Aged red wines should be opened fifteen to thirty minutes prior to serving to allow volatile acids to escape. The flavor and bouquet will improve tremendously. All wines must be handled gently. A table wine loses a lot of its flavor and bouquet when it is shaken and roughened up. It takes hours to regain its composure and restore its flavor and bouquet.

If it is a white or rosé wine or champagne, it should be served chilled. When the server removes the bottle from the wine cooler, it will be dripping. Have a serviette to dry the bottle. If the bottle is not empty after pouring, it is returned to the wine cooler so the wine will remain chilled. When the bottle is empty, it is put in the wine cooler upside down, in other words, with the neck of the bottle toward the bottom of the cooler. There is a chance that the host, noticing that the bottle is empty, might order another.

A serviette is used to prevent dripping of the wine, but it is not wrapped around the bottle. The label, which depicts the host's choice, should be exposed at all times and held so he and his guests can see it as the wine is being poured.

A small amount of wine should be poured into the glass of the host for his approval before serving the other guests. A wine glass should never be more than one-third to three-quarters full depending upon the size of the glass. One-third for the very large glass, one-half for the medium size, and three-quarters for the small glass. It is important to use a large glass if possible— it captures the bouquet better and is far more festive.

The neck of the bottle should not touch the glass. Not only is it considered improper, but many people are sensitive about anything touching the rim of their glass, even the neck of a bottle that has been thoroughly cleaned.

The wine complements the food and makes it more palatable, but added to the ritual of a nicely presented wine— the bottle properly opened, and wine well-served—it becomes a performance that transforms mere eating into the fascinating world of dining.

The most famed restaurants in the world are noted for their wines as well as for their foods. That is because food is at its best when served with wine. Among all the common beverages of mankind, table wine is the only one that is exclusively a mealtime beverage. Wine is also the "festive" beverage and its service often marks a very special occasion. Because it is made to go with food, wine is not competitive with other beverages. Its only competition is ice water which impairs mealtime enjoyment and is costly when you take into consideration that ninety-nine out of a hundred beverage spills are water.

Members who buy cocktails before the meal many times also buy wine with the meal.

Serving champagne or other "sparkling wines" is different. The cork is covered with foil under which is a wire loop, twisted so it keeps the cork from coming out. The foil capsule and the wire can usually be removed at one time by untwisting the wire loop and pulling the foil and the wire off together. The thumb should be held on top of the cork to keep it from popping out unexpectedly. It is very seldom that this would happen but occasionally it does. It is better to be safe.

The cork of a bottle of champagne is not pulled but eased out. Actually, the easiest way is to place a serviette over the cork and top of the bottle, hold it and the cork which is in it firmly in the left hand and gently twist the bottle with the right hand, working the cork out. This is the way to do it if the servers are right-handed. Reverse the position if they are left-handed. The cork must be held tightly so it doesn't jar loose and hit someone. Plastic corks, particularly, have a habit of being unpredictable. To permit the cork to make a loud "pop" is festive and possibly preferable, but for afficionados who really know their champagne and want it served at the peak of perfection, the cork should be removed so the least possible amount of gas escapes.

To pour champagne, the server starts in the same manner as with "still wine"—first a little in the host's glass for his approval, then proceeding to fill the glasses of the others. There is a slight difference between the pouring of still wine and the pouring of champagne. Champagne very often bubbles up in the glass when it is first poured, creating somewhat of a foam, which takes a few moments to disappear. The servers proceed to the next glass and to the others around the table. By that time, the foam in the first glass will have dissipated and the filling can be completed.

When refilling the glasses, train the server to equalize the amount in each glass so there is enough wine for all instead of pouring so much in a few glasses that the bottle is empty just before reaching the last glass.

The managers check off list for wine promotion is:

1. Have a good up-to-date, attractive wine list. If a new one is being prepared use some showmanship and imagination. Here are some ideas for the list.
   - Use the word American (never domestic) for our wines.
   - Assign a number to each of the wines. Coordinate this number with the bin card and the new menu.
   - Group the wines into the five classes. Have a good American as well as imported in each class.
   - Add a brief description for each wine listed, such as:

   Cabernet Sauvignon A strong, full-bodied red wine with a fruity, grape flavor. Just great with steak.

   - Price wines to achieve the same percentage of profit as on food.
   - Stock and refrigerate, as necessary, those wines on the list.
2. Have the proper wine-serving gear.
   - Each server must have a good corkscrew and practice using it.
   - Wine buckets to keep white and sparkling wines chilled are a necessity.
3. Put wine glasses on every table as part of the normal setup for dinner.
4. Build a wine display in the dining room.
5. Advertise the complete wine service and fine wine list in every media that is available. The monthly bulletin could feature the "Wine of the Month." Use the wineries to assist with attractive cuts, etc. Take exerpts, such as the section on "Appetizer Wines," and run a monthly feature article from the text. Use verbatim information from this text to fashion attractive table tents.

PROMOTING THE COCKTAIL LOUNGE AND BAR

As in all club promotions the basic theme is to start by supplying everything the competing commercial establishments have and going on from there. Some of these are:

1. Stock foreign beers. Most wholesale beverage dealers stock beers from:

Germany	Japan
Holland	Australia
Czechoslovakia	Mexico
Norway	Greece
Poland	Portugal
Denmark	Scotland
Ireland	England

Some specialty houses also stock many more. A club could specialize in imported beers with an investment in a beer cooler, less than a $250 inventory, and offer at least fifteen varieties of imported beer. All of the dealers will sell one case and many will sell just one six pack. The sale of these is promoted with a special menu and advertised by all the methods at the club's disposal.

2. Allow members to pay just one check regardless of how long they stay or how many drinks they have. Called "running a tab," cocktail servers fight this as it cuts down severely on their tips. Clubs who change from a "pay as you order" to a "running tab" can make this more palatable to the employees by adding a service charge to the check.

3. Have a cocktail menu. This is an item that must be done on a magnificent scale or not at all. The menu should be glossy, have pictures, and feature exotic drinks. The club should be the only place within its marketing area that prepares certain drinks.

4. Dress up the staff. There is no one right way to costume the cocktail and bar staff but there are certain general rules that, if followed, create the "club atmosphere." The manager need not think of the word "uniform" in its literal sense, in that all the servers need not be dressed the same. The uniform must make the employee feel comfortable. Any uniform that might cause the employee embarrassment is a no-no. If possible, have the uniform in keeping with the decor of the room and give each employee some individuality—a different color, a different way to tie a scarf or apron, ascots instead of ties. Provide for cocktail service anyplace in the club that the members desire it. And have a system so that diners can have a cocktail in the lounge while awaiting dinner

Jogging

service. If the member has not finished his or hers when the table is ready it should be carried by a member of the staff from the lounge to the dining room table.

PROMOTING SPORTS

The responsibility for promoting the sports activities of the club should be delegated to the professionals who head the various divisions. The promotion is primarily done through programs and each division head should be made responsible for producing one each quarter. Planning should begin at least sixty days in advance. A longer lead time may be necessary for major events but two months should be the minimum.

Promotions that are absolutely essential are tournaments, start-up, and season's end banquets. These should always be affairs that are looked forward to with great anticipation and pleasure by the members. Management must make every effort to make these the fun parties the members enjoy. In many clubs, the banquets are the high points of the social year.

Management must be alert to the member's desires in the sports area. All too frequently the lines of communication do not include the manager and it is very important that the professional division-heads work for and with the manager. Some examples of what managers must watch for are:

- professionals too busy playing their specialty to provide adequate time for lessons
- no lessons for young players
- inadequate programs for novices because the committees are all proficient
- technical problems with the courses, courts, or pools that are handled as "crisis" by the staff
- arrangements between professionals of one club with professionals of other clubs excluding management

REVIEW QUESTIONS

1. Discuss the needs for advertising in the private club business.
2. Discuss the various methods that can be used to increase the member's use of the dining rooms.
3. Discuss how a Valentine's Day dinner and dance would be advertised, promoted, and merchandised.
4. Discuss and summarize those details of wine service a manager should know.
5. Discuss and evaluate the need of a wine list as part of the menu and as a separate one.

8

Entertainment

OVERVIEW

The aims of this chapter are to explain in depth the two broad categories of club entertainment.

The controls that management must maintain are described and practical methods of application are explained.

The chapter will give the necessary knowledge so that the proper financial balance between entertainment and profit can be maintained.

PURPOSE

The purpose of club entertainment is to get the members to use the facilities. In order to do this it must amuse, divert, give pleasure to the members, and be vivid enough to be remembered. It is "fond memories" that bring the members back. Every big affair the club has should have a souvenir for the member to take home.

Entertainment can be divided into two broad types: in-house and external. Entertainment that is in-house is completely self contained as regards personnel. Equipment may be rented or purchased, but the members or club staff provide the people needed. The external type means that persons other than members and staff provide it.

The types and styles of entertainment that can be offered to club members are limitless. There is apparently no clearly defined established pattern to guide management such as age, social position, profession, education, sex, or ethnic background. However there are certain considerations that may be helpful.

Age The ages at the two ends of the spectrum are the most difficult to satisfy. The teenage is complicated because the span of variety is limited, much of the music is "fad," and it is part of the status game to dance and listen only to an "in" group. In all teenage planning have a good representation of youngsters on the committee. The older members are often more interested in their own conversation than in dancing, and any music is almost an annoyance. The manager explains this to the reservation clerk so that tables at a distance from the band or in another room may be offered.

Social position, profession, and education All these aspects play a part if they have added to the individual's social experience. This means some members will have been exposed to more clubs, fine restaurants, theatres, and good hotels than the average member and therefore can make valid comparisons.

Sex Top clubs are finding that more and more couples, regardless of age, are spending more time together. Even that surefire female standby, the fashion show, attracts couples. It would be smart to aim the bulk of the entertainment package at them.

Ethnic Background There are never any problems with ethnic entertainment as long as all or none of the members have strong ethnic ties. It is gauche to have "A Night in Old . . . " such and such a place or country. Today party themes are specific such as fiestas, bazaars, carnivals, festivals, galas, celebrations, fetes, jubilees, and reveleries.

ORGANIZATION

The entertainment that is offered by the club is the acid test of the manager's imagination and professionalism. All entertainment is budgeted and approved by the various club committees but the success or failure of any facet of the club's business is the manager's sole responsibility. A successful program embodies the following steps:

1. The Idea—A program does not have to be completely new to be different. A twist to an old idea might be very popular. For example, many managers are content with the club's New Year's Party that consists of some food, a flood of alcoholic beverages, a band, and some party favors. Then the manager will take reservations and set the tables so that parties can be formed. Some members will like this, many will be bored, many came once, and many never attend. The reason of course is that management has clearly indicated that there is no involvement, the toy's are furnished but the members must amuse themselves. There are many ways management can get involved, such as setting a theme party with the manager being one of the star performers. Party ideas are judged on whether or not they are new to the manager's club members, not whether or not they are new. CMAA publishes a Book on party ideas and each month in their magazine have a write-up, with details of parties.

2. Planning—The planning for any entertainment includes three stages:

   a. *What the club is going to do.* This includes the broad scope of the event
      - what it is
      - the theme if any
      - day, date, and time
      - ingredients
        Advertising
        Other printed materials
        Decorations
        Music
        Special props
        Special food and drinks
        Price

   b. *How the club will do it.* Will a committee handle the event? This could be an existing one or one formed specifically for the event. Also consideration must be given to whether the staff can handle it better themselves.

   c. *Who will be responsible for what.* The manager breaks down the tasks that need to be accomplished into division components and assigns the duties to those individuals responsible.

3. Implementation—It is now the manager's responsibility to follow through to insure each of the tasks assigned are accomplished.

IN-HOUSE ENTERTAINMENT

The inhouse entertainment provided by the club can be divided into the built-in and special.

Built-in Entertainment

This kind of amusement is available to the members at all times the club is open and can be seasonal as well as year-round. These are:

1. Outdoors facilities—the golf course, tennis courts and pools.
2. Television facilities—the set could be in the bar, reading room, or have a space of its own. Some clubs are having some success purchasing or renting large-screen sets for major television events.
3. Game devices—these would include pool and billiard tables, slot and pinball machines, shuffleboard, air hockey and ping pong tables, electronic games, etc. These could be placed throughout the club or confined to special rooms.
4. Card, reading, and writing rooms
5. Library
6. Weather station—a push-button weather radio station would be very useful to a club that has both indoor and outdoor activities. They are relatively inexpensive for the service they provide, and do not need an antenna.
7. Ticker-tape machine—a ticker tape machine that quotes stock market prices can be leased for a very modest price. The installation is via telephone lines and is not expensive or complicated. The only problem is that it is noisy and should be installed where this would not be an annoyance.

Special Entertainment

This is the one-time or cycle event that is completely self-contained. The personnel involved are the members and the staff. These entertainments include the following:

1. Bingo, Keno or other games—the motion picture race games have become popular and satisfy some segment of the clubs membership. The race games come under many names. A few of the best known are Armchair Races, Cinema Races, A Night at the Races.

2. Member and staff entertainment—the talent is there, it just takes a lot of work by management to uncover it. The normal club members are gregarious and this means there is some amount of "ham" in their makeup. Management may be able to start a drama, prose or poetry-reading club by just providing interest and rehearsal space. Musicians are discovered through conversation. Classes in dancing, art, and crafts may be of interest to the members. These cannot be formed by questionnaires—management must take the initiative and discover the interests and talent personally. Then management has a pool of special entertainment such as

- A play or musical
- A pantomime show
- A trio or band
- Vocalists or soloists
- Prose or poetry readers

PERFORMANCE BONDS, CONTRACTS, AND LIABILITY

This covers any type of entertainment that includes hiring personnel other than the club staff. It may be an orchestra, band, combo, show, discotheque entertainer, go-go dancers, etc. This type of entertainment always requires a written contract between the club and personnel involved, a performance bond, and an understanding of the liability for tort acts of the entertainer and his staff.

Contract

A written contract with the entertainer or agent will not, in itself, guarantee a successful performance but it is a start. It puts the parties on notice that the club expects certain things that, if done, will result in the payment of the amount stipulated in advance. The specifics of the contract follow:

1. Date of the contract, the place of performance, the time, day, and date of the performance, and provisions as to the penalties for lateness.

2. The length of the performance—one, two, or more hours.

3. The exact name of the entertainment group, the names of persons involved, and a picture of the persons who will be performing at the club—it is too late to take action if the management thinks they are hiring a name band and only the leader shows up on the performance night with a picked up local group.

4. If a band is being contracted, the exact number of minutes they will play each hour.

5. What equipment the club must furnish—some dinner-theatre shows have a mass of equipment to move.

6. Will any transportation be needed for the performance.

7. Food, drinks, and lodging for the performers.

8. How will payment be made.

9. How contractual disputes are handled—the club manager, who signs the contract, will be the final arbitrator in all disputes.

10. To require a performance bond—this is an insurance policy, purchased by the entertainer, that guarantees that he will appear at the time, date, and place specified or the club will be reimbursed for their loss. An easy way to enforce this requirement is to pay an advance deposit. It is an essential part of the contract as some performers schedule their appearances so close together, not allowing sufficient time for travel delays, that the club can be seriously inconvenienced.

11. The conduct of the entertainers must remain subject to the control of the club manager at all times. The contract should specify that:

    • Food and drink are not allowed on the bandstand.

    • Smoking is not permitted on the bandstand.

    • All personnel must conform to the dress rules of the club, except while in costume.

    • All personnel must at all times conduct themselves as ladies and gentlemen.

    • Drunkenness and/or the use of any narcotics or hallucinatory drugs is a just cause for cancelling the contract with no reimbursement.

12. The management reserves the right to control the volume of sound of any and all pieces of electronic amplifying equipment.

13. The management reserves the right to insist that no lyrics, movements, or gestures be indecent, obscene, or in poor taste.

14. The principal entertainer must carry liability insurance to protect the club from any injuries that may result from the act either to the actor, club member, club guest, or club employee.

15. The contract can be terminated, without penalty, by the club until twenty-four hours before the performance is scheduled if for any reason the club cannot stage the act.

MANAGEMENT CONTROL OF ENTERTAINERS

The manager must exercise the most careful judgment in the control of entertainers because of the fine line between employees and contractors. If detailed supervision is given, the entertainer could become an employee under Internal Revenue regulations and the club would then be responsible for withholding tax, FICA, workman's compensation, and other taxes. The manager must have a very complete idea of the performance to be given and while the contract is fairly complete, not all details are ever covered. For example, if the band is very versatile, does management want their entire repertoire? Will the club members like funky rock, western, hill-billy, etc? It just may be that they don't particularly care for the smooth, syrupy sounds of the '40s either. Management must know what the members like, from personal contact with them, and make certain that their wishes are followed. A very modern show might be acceptable on Broadway and in poor taste at the club. Nudity may or may not offend the members. If dinner is being served at six and live music is scheduled at eight in the same room, then management should strive to set the band up at five. If this is not possible then perhaps they could be persuaded to at least tune their instruments in another room. Some groups, unless controlled, will disrupt a very nice dinner atmosphere.

All or most of these details can be part of the contract and then can be better controlled. However, by paying for the entertainment, management acquires the right to stage it for the best presentation to the members. Live entertainment is being replaced by electronic gadgetry in America and the manager who can afford the expense of performers has leverage that was never possible in the past.

IDEAS

Entertainment ideas need not be completely new as mentioned previously, but can be an old plan with a new twist. For example, a theme party for New Year's Eve. When one manager approached the board of directors with this idea they were delighted. The club didn't need any additional business, New Year's Eve was always a sellout. But the manager thought that the members might have more fun if they dressed up. It was a smashing success and is an excellent illustration of "involved" management. The manager's idea was to celebrate 1900, the turn of the century, instead of the actual year. The members were encouraged to wear appropriate costumes (which they did) and the theme carried throughout the club.

The ideas for the entertainment of the members come from many places:

1. The Commerce Publishing Company reprints the best ideas presented by members of the CMAA, from *Club Management* magazine. These are sold by CMAA in pamphlet form for a very nominal price. The pamphlets are called "Ideas for Parties."
2. The club purveyors are another fine source of party ideas:
   - U.S. Brewer's Association has a free booklet, "Beer Party USA," available through local beer distributors.
   - Most distillers publish one or more party idea books.
   - Boyles of Kansas City has a party book, as do many other meat and specialty houses.
3. Marketing (ideas in disguise) plans are available from many equipment manufacturers.
4. The National Restaurant Association has a booklet entitled "Ideas for Profit for Food Service Operators." Two new ideas that may be pleasing to the members are:
   - Have a teenage party at the same time as the grown-up one. Invite the local high school band as guests of honor to promenade in uniform through the adults' ballroom and put on a show, then to the teenagers' party where they are VIPS.

Playgrounds

- Have a theme party to celebrate the birthday or to honor some great Mexican, frontierman, Japanese, Chinese, Filipino, Spaniard, Italian, or German. The dates and names can be found in many encyclopedias.

FINANCIAL ANALYSIS

The purpose of a good entertainment program is to cultivate the membership and increase business at a predetermined profit or loss. The manager must be able to analyze the financial impact of the affairs. Too many times when additional profit is needed, entertainment is engaged without this knowledge.

One easy way to compute the dollars involved is to use the gross-profit percentage generated by a particular division. Then the manager can know when the dollar sales become profit.

The food department works on a 5 percent net profit, the bar on 25 percent. A dinner dance is planned. The additional costs are represented by the band and club labor needed to rearrange the room and cleanup. This is computed to be $750.00.

The bar may conservatively plan on selling two drinks for every additional diner. The food check average is $10.00 per person, the two drinks $3.00. Therefore $1.25 profit can be expected from each member at the dance:

$$5\% \text{ of } 10.00 = .50 + 25\% \text{ of } \$3.00 = .75 \text{ for a total of } 1.25$$

If the normal dinner crowd is 100 then 600 additional diners would be needed to break even:

$$\$750.00 \div \$1.25 = 600 \text{ members.}$$

Thus entertainment, per se, may not be the answer for more profit. Perhaps a package deal could be established so that part of the cost would be paid by all diners. If the event attracted 100 additional diners the $125.00 (100 × 1.25 = $125.00) with the costs at $750.00 could be generated if each of the 200 members were charged $3.125 admission (perhaps as a cover charge). The club would then break even. Any amount charged in addition to this would be a profit.

The manager must perform similar analyses on every event, whether it is in the clubhouse or an athletic tournament, to learn whether the club can make a profit, break even, or that the event must be subsidized.

REVIEW QUESTIONS

1. Discuss the process used in selecting the "right" entertainment for the club.
2. Discuss the methods that can then be used to procure and control that entertainment.
3. Discuss the contractual steps that might be necessary if a big-name entertainer were being considered for a performance.
4. Discuss the methods that management must use and the research of fiscal facts needed to plan financially viable entertainment.
5. Discuss the sources of entertainment ideas and develop at least one of your own.

Epilogue

The position of club manager is the most difficult in the hospitality industry. The skills required to operate a modern club successfully are a combination of those needed in hotels, restaurants, night clubs, cocktail lounges, theatres, retail stores, and major sporting promotion. The club business therefore is "different."

The five ways in which it is "different" from segments of other businesses are:

1. A club has an established, never-changing clientele. There is no other business that must cope with the same customer on its premises for the same products day after day, week after week, month after month, and year after year.
2. The club members pay for the privilege (through dues) of purchasing the products offered.
3. The manager of a club is expected to know more about the business than the owners. Their operations knowledge (the owners) can be equated with that of the stock holders of a very large corporation.
4. Making a profit may not be a management objective. Other objectives of the commercial hospitality business may have very different priorities in a club.
5. In club operations the manager will almost always get an opportunity to use the total knowledge of the hospitality business that has been learned both academically and from experience.

This completes the text. For those managers who have been patient and interested enough to read these words, and for management personnel in all clubs, I have taken the liberty of rephrasing an old Irish saying:

> May the road rise up to meet you
> And the wind be at your back,
> The sun shine warm upon your face
> Thine fields, for rain, ne'er lack,
> May your heart be filled with glory
> As each day's task you do;
> Your hand go out to all mankind
> As God's goes out to you.

Index